DUTCH OVEN

COOKBOOK

100 Recipes for Your Most Versatile Pot,

Including Breakfast, Meat, Soups, Sides,

Desserts, Sandwiches, and More.

By Leslie Hanks

INTRODUCTION

A Dutch oven is a large, heavy pot with a tight-fitting lid that is rather shallow. The only pots that can be considered Dutch ovens aren't the enameled cast iron casseroles with two tiny handles and a lid, as we often assume. The most crucial characteristics of a Dutch oven are its weight, which is necessary to maintain a steady temperature for an extended period of time in the oven or on the stove, and its tight-fitting cover, which keeps heat inside the pot.

Cooking shows, shopping networks, and the internet all expose home chefs to what might seem like an infinite variety of cookware—different materials, different patterns, and different parts. Some experienced cooks buy a lot of cookware, while others don't, but they all recognize the importance of having a small number of truly dependable, multipurpose tools.

One such item is the Dutch oven. In fact, some people contend that it is the only pot you will ever need. Cooks rely on it to make an incredible variety of dishes, from braising to slow-cooking stews to soups. Dutch ovens often have flat bottoms and loop handles, and they always include lids. Their capacities range from two to thirteen quarts, and they are roughly four to five inches deep. Your kitchen's Dutch oven will enable you to prepare delicious meals that will astound your entire family.

The truth is that a Dutch oven can be used to cook anything in a pot.

Since a Dutch oven is heavy and has a tight-fitting cover, you may cook in an oven set to 300 degrees Fahrenheit or on a stovetop over a low flame without the cooking liquid draining before the meat is cooked and tender. In a similar spirit, soups and stews, which take a while to cook on the stove, are frequently prepared in Dutch ovens.

Typically composed of cast iron, enameled Dutch ovens can reach extremely high temperatures and retain heat effectively, making them ideal for searing a variety of meals, including meats and vegetables.

The most well-known application of a Dutch oven is probably for making bread. To produce a crisp crust on rustic bread, heat retention and a tight lid are essential. The nicest crust is created by the steam that remains in the pan when the lid is on.

Dutch ovens are excellent for braises, stews, sauces, soups, and other moist-heat cooking techniques. A dish or a whole chicken can be prepared in this pot. Alternatively, you can transfer your pot to the oven to finish cooking after browning the meat and vegetables on the stove and letting them simmer. Additionally, Dutch ovens are the preferred cooking appliances for sourdough and no-knead bread.

TABLE OF CONTENTS

CHAPTER 1: BREAKFAST

DUTCH OVEN CHEESY BACON WITH EGGS

Total Time: 1 hr. 5 min

Prep time: 40 min.

Cook time: 25 min.

Servings: 8

INGREDIENTS

- 1 pound of diced bacon strips.
- O'Brien's hash brown potatoes, 1 package (20 oz.), refrigerated.
- 8 big eggs.
- Half-and-half cream, 1/2 cup.
- 1⁄2 to 1 teaspoon of spicy sauce
- 2 cups of shredded Monterey Jack and cheddar cheese.

INSTRUCTION

1. Use 32–36 charcoal briquettes or large wood chips to prepare a bonfire or grill for medium–high heat.
2. Cook bacon until crisp in a 10-inch Dutch oven over a campfire, tossing periodically. Utilize a slotted spoon to remove and drain on paper towels. Drippings are discarded, leaving 2 tablespoons in the pan.
3. Potatoes should be gently pressed into the Dutch oven's bottom and 1 inch up its side. Eggs, cream, and, if desired, pepper sauce should be combined in a small basin. Pour over potatoes and top with cheese and fried bacon.
4. Dutch oven cover Place Dutch oven on top of 16–18 briquettes until they are completely covered in white ash or wood chips. 16–18 briquettes should be placed on the pan cover using long-handled tongs.
5. Cook for 20 to 25 minutes, or until cheese has melted and the eggs are fully set. Use tongs to carefully lift the cover to see if the food is done. Cook for a further five minutes if necessary.

SAUSAGE AND EGGS OVER CHEDDAR

Prep: 20 Min.

Cook Time: 20 Min.

Servings: 6

INGREDIENTS

- 1 lb. of bulk Italian sausage.
- 1 chopped large sweet onion.
- 1 chopped medium-sized sweet yellow pepper.
- 1 chopped medium-sized sweet red pepper.
- 6 cups of water.
- 1-1/2 cups of quick-cooking grits.
- 1 cup of sharp cheddar cheese, shredded.
- 1/2 cup of Parmesan cheese, shredded.
- half-and-half Cream, 2 tbsp.
- 1/2 tsp of salt.
- 1/4 tsp of pepper.
- 2 tsp of olive oil.
- 6 eggs.
- spicy pepper sauce.

INSTRUCTION

1. With the sausage broken up into crumbles, sauté the sausage, onion, yellow pepper, and red pepper in a Dutch oven over medium heat for 6 to 8 minutes, or until the vegetables are tender and the sausage has lost its pink color. Drain.
2. Bring water to a boil in a big saucepan in the meantime. Stir the grits in gradually. Reduce heat to medium-low; simmer, covered, for about 5 minutes, stirring periodically, until thickened. Get rid of the heat. Add the cheeses, the cream, the salt, and the pepper, and stir.

3. Heat oil to medium-high heat in a large skillet. One at a time, crack eggs into the pan and turn heat to low. Cook, if desired, rotating once, until whites are set and yolks start to thicken. In six serving bowls, divide the grits; add the sausage mixture and the eggs on top. Serve with pepper sauce, if preferred.

SCRAMBLED EGG BREAD

Prep: 25 min.

Cook: 10 min.

Servings: 4

INGREDIENTS

- 1 loaf of unsliced French bread, 1 pound.
- 2 tbsp of butter, softened and divided.
- 2 tbsp butter, divided.
- 1 chopped small onion.
- 1 cup fully cooked cubed ham
- 1 large tomato, cut into pieces.
- 6 eggs.
- 1/8 tsp of pepper.
- 1 1/2 cups of divided cheddar cheese shreds.

INSTRUCTION

1. Set up a grill or a campfire for medium heat. Each piece of bread should first be divided in half crosswise, then lengthwise. Hollow out two sections, leaving shells that are 1/2 in. Cube the removed bread and set aside 1-1/2 cups (save remaining cubes for another use). Over the bread shells, spread 1 tablespoon of softened butter. Over the remaining bread halves, spread the remaining softened butter. Place aside.
2. Over a campfire, melt 1 tablespoon of butter in a small Dutch oven. Add the onion and stir for 3 to 4 minutes, or until it is soft. Add tomato and ham; stir; then take out of pan.
3. Combine the eggs and pepper in a small bowl. Heat the remaining butter in the same pan. Pour in the egg mixture and cook and stir it until there is no longer any liquid egg. Add the ham mixture, a cup of cheese, and the bread cubes you set aside. Fill bread shells with contents and top with remaining cheese. Transfer to a disposable 13 x 9-inch foil pan and wrap with foil.

4. Pan over the campfire Cook for 8 to 10 minutes, or until cheese has completely melted. Toast reserved bread halves for one to two minutes with the butter side down. Toast each egg bread piece, then cut each piece in half.

HONEY BAGELS

Prep: 1 hour + standing

Bake: 20 min.

Makes: 1 dozen

INGREDIENTS

- 1 tbsp dry active yeast.
- 1-1/4 cups of heated (110–115°) water.
- Canola oil, 3 tsp.
- 3 tbsp. sugar.
- 3 tbsp. plus 1/4 cup of honey, divided.
- brown sugar, 1 tsp.
- Salt, 1 1/2 tsp.
- 1 large egg, at room temperature.
- bread flour, 4 to 5 cups.
- 1 tbsp of minced dry onion.
- 1 tsp. sesame seeds.
- 1 tbsp of poppy seeds.

INSTRUCTION

1. Warm water and yeast should be dissolved in a big bowl. Mix well after adding the oil, sugar, 3 tablespoons of honey, brown sugar, salt, and egg. To create a soft dough, stir with just enough flour.
2. Turn onto a floured surface and knead for 8 to 10 minutes, or until a smooth, firm dough forms. Cover and allow to rest for 10 minutes.
3. Put down the dough. 12 balls should be formed. To create a 1-1/2-inch hole, insert your thumb through each center. Dough can be shaped and stretched into even rings. Lie down on a floured surface. After ten minutes of resting undercover, slightly flatten the bagels.

4. Bring the remaining honey and 8 cups of water to a boil in a big pot or Dutch oven. Place one baguette at a time into the boiling water. Cook bagels for a further 45 seconds after turning. With a slotted spoon, remove bagels; drain; and top with poppy, sesame, and onion powder.

5. On parchment-lined baking pans, space bagels 2 inches apart. 12 minutes of baking at 425 degrees. About 5 more minutes of baking after turning the baking sheet.

BREAKFAST BURRITO RECIPE

Prep Time: 5 Mins

Cook Time: 20 Mins

Total Time: 25 Mins

Servings: 4

INGREDIENTS

- 1/2 pound of chorizo bulk sausage, pork.
- 4 beaten eggs.
- 1/4 tsp of salt.
- 1/8 tsp. pepper
- 1/2 cup of cheddar cheese, shredded.
- 4 tortillas flour.
- 4 tbsp of sour cream.
- 1 small bunch chopped cilantro

INSTRUCTION

1. Get your 10-inch cast iron camp Dutch oven ready for cooking. A campfire, camp stove, RV stove, or charcoal briquettes can all be used to prepare this dish.
2. Prepare the fresh herbs and weigh out all the ingredients.
3. Fry the sausage until it is thoroughly cooked over medium heat on a campfire or camp stove, crumbling it as it cooks. Cooking tip for the outdoors: Chorizo sausage, which contains a variety of spices, adds a ton of flavor with little work. However, the reddish-brown seasonings can trick you into thinking the sausage is fully cooked when it is actually undercooked.
4. In a bowl, combine the eggs, salt, and pepper
5. Before adding the eggs, lower the heat to a low setting. Camp Cooking Tip: Simply take out as many coals as are required to reduce the heat when cooking over a campfire or using charcoal briquettes. Simply turn the knob downward if you are using a propane stove to cook. It won't be an instantaneous heat drop, but keep in mind that cast iron equipment holds heat for longer lengths of time than other camp cookware materials.

6. Gently stir the egg mixture into the sausage-filled pot, then stir it again until the eggs are nearly set.
7. The cheese should now be added, and you should keep stirring until it melts.
8. As you spread the mixture onto the tortillas, split it up equally. then sprinkle cilantro and sour cream on top.
9. Enjoy by rolling the tortillas into burritos.

NOTE

- You can increase the serving size of this dish as needed. A 10-inch Dutch oven is a wonderful size to manage up to 4 meals, but if you're scaling for more, you'll need to raise the Dutch oven's size for optimum cooking.

DUTCH OVEN POTATOES

Prep: 20 min

Cook: 30 min

Yield: 4 to 6 servings

INGREDIENTS

- 1/4 pound of bacon (cut into 1-inch pieces).
- 1 chopped small onion.
- 2 1/2 pounds of russet potatoes, peeled and cut into bite-size chunks.
- 14 cup of parsley leaves, chopped.
- 1 tbsp. of seasoned salt.
- fresh-ground black pepper.
- 1/2 cup of water
- 2 tbsp. of small pieces butter.

INSTRUCTION

1. Heat a wood fire or an outside charcoal grill to medium.
2. In a Dutch oven positioned on the grill grate or directly on the embers, roast bacon until it is crisp. About 5 minutes after adding the onions, they should be translucent.
3. Put potatoes in a sizable bowl for mixing. Add the parsley and a pinch or two of salt and pepper. Mix each component thoroughly. Butter and water are added to the Dutch oven along with the potatoes. Cook potatoes for about 20 minutes, covered, until they are browned and soft. Warmly serve.

DUTCH OVEN BREAKFAST CASSEROLE

Prep Time: 20 Minutes

Cook Time: 30 Minutes

Total Time: 50 Minutes

Servings: 8

INGREDIENTS

- 3 cups of hash browns
- 16 oz of crumbled fresh sausage.
- 6 beaten eggs.
- 1 cup of grated cheddar cheese.
- biscuit dough for 6 biscuits.
- 4 tbsp of oil or butter.

INSTRUCTION

1. The Dutch oven should be preheated over a campfire or grate.
2. In the Dutch oven, add the sausage and half the butter or oil. Cook the sausage while stirring frequently until browned. Take out of the oven, then leave aside.
3. With the remaining butter or oil, add the hash browns. Brown one side before flipping.
4. Over the hash browns, re-layer the cooked sausage.
5. The sausage will trickle down into all the bottom layers, so add the beaten eggs on top of the sausage.
6. On top of the egg, grate some cheese.
7. Spread large spoonsful of biscuit dough evenly over the top of the eggs.
8. Make sure the Dutch oven lid fits tightly around the top before placing it. Place the Dutch oven right in the campfire, away from the flames, over some smoldering coals. Place four to eight huge, burning embers atop the lid.
9. Make sure there aren't any ash leaks into the food when you open the lid of the oven by periodically checking and rotating it.

10. When the biscuits are golden brown and fluffy on the inside, breakfast is finished. As a dish, cut out large chunks.

DUTCH OVEN CARROT CAKE

Prep Time: 15 Mins

Cook Time: 40 Mins

Total Time: 55 Mins

Servings: 8

INGREDIENTS

Ingredients of Carrot Cake:

- 1 1/2 cups of sugar in granules.
- 1 cup of vegetable oil
- 3 beaten eggs.
- 1 tsp of vanilla extract.
- 2 cups of all-purpose flour
- 2 tsp of cinnamon powder.
- 1 tsp. of baking soda.
- 1/2 a tsp of salt.
- 3 cups of medium carrots, shredded.
- 1 cup of raisins.
- 1 cup of pecans, coarsely chopped.

Ingredients of cream cheese Frosting:

- 8 ounces of softened cream cheese.
- 1 tsp of vanilla bean extract.
- Powdered sugar, 4 cups.

INSTRUCTION

1. 350 degrees should be reached in a 12-inch cast iron camp Dutch oven with the standard depth (17 top coals and 8 bottom coals).
2. Hand combines sugar, oil, eggs, and vanilla in a large bowl until well combined.

3. Mix the flour, baking soda, cinnamon, and salt in a medium basin until thoroughly combined.

4. Once all of the dry ingredients have been incorporated into the batter, start adding small quantities of the flour mixture to the wet ingredients while stirring.

5. Add the carrots, nuts, and raisins after that, and whisk everything together slowly. The simplest way to get carrots is pre-shredded, but utilizing a box grater at the campground makes it simple to physically shred carrots.

6. Pour the batter into the parchment paper at the bottom of the Dutch oven after lining it with parchment paper. Smooth the batter around a little to ensure that it is distributed evenly.

7. A toothpick put into the center of the cake should come out clean after baking at 350 degrees under the oven lid with 17 coals on top and 8 coals below. Although baking times may differ, this cake should be ready in 40 to 45 minutes.

8. Cooking tip for the outdoors: Rotate the oven and cover in opposition while the carrot cake bakes. For a lovely, uniformly baked and browned cake, rotate the pan by 1/4 turn every 10 to 15 minutes during baking. With the help of the parchment paper liner's "handles," remove the cake from the oven and place it aside to cool completely before icing and serving.

9. Cream cheese and vanilla are added to the bottom of a big bowl to make the cream cheese icing while the cake cools. The easiest technique to prepare frosting without an electric mixer is to "smash" the vanilla into the cream cheese with a fork.

10. With a fork, "smash" the powdered sugar into the cream cheese mixture as you add it, a little at a time. Alternatively, you can use a dough cutter to combine these ingredients.

11. Since the frosting will be thick, use a knife to spread it on the top and sides of the cake in multiple thin layers. Applying this thick frosting is made simpler by piping it from a plastic food bag. See how to achieve that in the short video below.

12. Serve this delicious sweet delicacy by slicing it. It is best to keep any leftovers in the fridge.

CINNAMON ROLLS WITH CREAM CHEESE ICING

Prep Time: 2 hrs. 30 mins

Cook Time: 25 mins

Total Time: 2 hrs. 55 mins

Servings: 16 rolls

INGREDIENTS

For the Cinnamon Rolls:

- Milk, 2 cups (473 ml) (I used whole milk).
- 1/2 cup of canola oil (118 ml) or olive or avocado oil.
- 1/2 cup of granulated sugar (100 gm).
- 2 and 1/4 tsp active dry yeast or instant yeast (one packet).
- 4 and 1/2 cups (562 gm) of all-purpose flour, divided.1.
- 1/2 teaspoon of baking powder
- 1/2 tsp of baking soda
- 1 1/2 tsp of salt.
- 1/2 cup (113 gm) of melted unsalted butter.
- 1 cup (150gm) of unpackaged brown sugar.
- Cinnamon, 2 tsp (as needed).

For the Cream Cheese Icing:

- 4 oz (113gm) of room temperature cream cheese
- 4 tbsp (56gm) softened unsalted butter
- 1 cup (113gm) of powdered sugar.
- 1 tsp vanilla bean paste or extract.
- A bit of salt.
- 1/4 cups of your preferred milk.

INSTRUCTIONS

For the Cinnamon Rolls:

1. I used a Dutch oven to combine the milk, oil, and sugar. Heat the mixture over medium heat until it is about to boil (or microwave this mixture in a large bowl until just before boiling). When the mixture is just warm to the touch, about 105-110 degrees F, turn off the heat and let it cool.

2. Let the yeast rest on top of the milk mixture for a couple of minutes. With a wooden spoon, add 4 cups (500gm) of the flour and stir until a dough that is uniformly integrated forms.

3. If your kitchen is cold, turn on the oven while the mixture is covered and let to rise for about an hour. Verify if it is rising after 30 minutes by checking. It ought to have doubled in size and begun to smell yeasty by the end of the hour.

4. Salt, baking soda, and the remaining 1/2 cup (62gm) of flour should be added at this point. Stir everything together until well-combined. The dough should not be sticky and should be simple to manage. If the dough is sticky, chill it for an hour; it should become considerably more malleable.

5. The dough should be divided in half, with one half being rolled out to a roughly 128-inch rectangle on a surface that has been WELL floured. Before rolling out the dough, it helps to flour the surface and your rolling pin to prevent sticking. On top of the dough, equally distribute half the melted butter, half the brown sugar, and half the cinnamon.

6. Roll the dough towards you, starting with the long edge that is furthest away from you. As you do so, move your fingers evenly back and forth along the dough. Place in a greased pie dish or 9-inch round cake pan, and then use a sharp knife or unflavored dental floss to cut into 8 equal rolls.

7. Utilizing the second half of the dough, repeat steps 5 and 6.

8. Set oven to 375 degrees Fahrenheit. While the oven heats up, leave the rolls to rise slightly on the counter for 15 to 20 minutes. Until golden brown, bake for 20 to 22 minutes. Make the cream cheese icing while the rolls are baking.

For the Cream Cheese Icing:

1. In a medium bowl, whisk cream cheese and butter until well blended and creamy. Once more mix in the salt and vanilla. Add the powdered sugar and mix well. When the mixture achieves a pourable but still thick consistency, add milk 1 tablespoon at a time.

2. Make sure the tops of the warm cinnamon buns in the pan are thoroughly covered by the icing by pouring and spreading it evenly over them. Serve warm with coffee and observe people's pure joy-filled eyes!

NOTES

- If there are any leftovers, place them in the refrigerator for up to 5 days. To reheat, simply microwave for 20 to 30 seconds.
- The cinnamon rolls can be prepared the night before through step 6 of the make-ahead instructions (shaping the rolls and placing in the pans). Overnight in the refrigerator, wrap pans with plastic wrap. Pans should be left out on the counter while the oven is preheating in the morning so that rolls can warm up before baking.
- The baked rolls can be frozen for up to three months if they are individually wrapped in plastic wrap and kept in a freezer bag. Simply reheat in a 250-degree oven for 15 minutes or for 30 seconds in a microwave.
- Dough that has been shaped and well-wrapped can be frozen for up to three months in a pan or another container. Before baking, leave them out on the counter for 2 hours to let them finish their second rise and reach room temperature. As indicated, bake.
- Oat milk has proven to be the best milk substitute in my experience. If using almond milk, add at least 1/4 cup more flour to the recipe to prevent a very sticky, unworkable dough.
- You may make just 8 cinnamon rolls from the entire recipe if you cut it in half. You simply need one pie dish or cake pan, and all the steps are the same.

POTATO AND HAM HASH

Prep: 15 mins

Cook: 10 mins

Total: 25 mins

Servings: 6

INGREDIENTS

- 3 tbsp of margarine or unsalted butter.
- 2 medium potatoes, cooked, cubed, and peeled.
- 1 small onion, cut finely.
- 1/2 of a green bell pepper, finely chopped.
- 1 cup of cooked ham, finely diced.
- 1/4 tsp salt, or as needed.
- 1/8 tsp of freshly ground black pepper.
- 1/4 tsp of crumbled dried thyme.

INSTRUCTION

1. assemble the ingredients.
2. In a large skillet over medium heat, melt the butter.
3. The diced potatoes, onions, bell pepper, and ham should be added once the butter has melted and ceased foaming. Mix well.
4. Cook the hash, tossing and flipping it regularly, until it is well-browned. Add the dried crushed thyme and season to taste with salt and freshly ground black pepper.
5. Tips
6. To expedite the preparation process and save time on the day of the meal, chop the vegetables, potatoes, and ham the night before. After cubing the potatoes, store them in water, then pat them dry before adding them to the skillet to cook. By doing this, the potatoes won't get brown.
7. For the hash, use frozen or thawed leftover boiled, seasoned potatoes.

DUTCH OVEN BACON SCRAMBLE

Prep Time: 10 Mins

Cook Time: 20 Mins

Total Time: 30 Mins

Servings: 2

INGREDIENTS

- 4 thick pieces of bacon, chopped.
- 1/2 small onion, chopped.
- 1 medium tomato, chopped
- 1 cup chopped fresh spinach.
- 4 beaten eggs.
- add salt and pepper as needed.
- 1/2 cup of cheddar cheese, shredded.

INSTRUCTIONS:

1. Get your 10-inch cast iron camp Dutch oven ready for cooking. A campfire, camp stove, RV stove, or charcoal briquettes can all be used to prepare this dish. See note in the section below.
2. Heat a 10-inch Dutch oven to a temperature of medium-high.
3. Cook the bacon in a skillet until almost done.
4. Add the onions now and stir while cooking until the onions are just beginning to soften.
5. Now it's time to add the spinach and cook it while stirring until it has wilted.
6. The tomatoes should only start to soften after being added and stirred in.
7. Before adding the eggs, lower the heat to a low setting. Camp Cooking Tip: Simply take out as many coals as are required to reduce the heat when cooking over a campfire or using charcoal briquettes. Simply turn the knob downward if you are using a propane stove to cook. It won't be an instantaneous heat drop, but keep in mind that cast iron equipment holds heat for longer lengths of time than other camp cookware materials.

8. Add the eggs once the heat has been decreased. as they cook, stirring constantly... To ensure that nothing sticks, you should work your way around the entire pan's bottom while scraping it.
9. Add the cheese to the bacon and egg mixture when the eggs are almost done. then heat with the lid off the Dutch oven until the cheese is melted and gooey. Enjoy a hot serving.

NOTES:

o   This dish can be scaled up as needed and serves two people. A 10-inch Dutch oven is a wonderful size to manage up to 4 meals, but if you're scaling for more, you'll need to raise the Dutch oven's size for optimum cooking.

CINNAMON BAKED FRENCH TOAST

Total Time: 13 hr.

Prep Time: 15 min

Inactive: 12 hr.

Cook Time: 45 min

Servings: 12

INGREDIENTS

French Toast:

- Using butter for Greasing.
- 1 loaf sourdough or crusty French bread
- 8 whole eggs.
- 2 cups of milk.
- 1/2 cup heavy whipping cream.
- 1/2 cup of granulated sugar.
- brown sugar, 1/2 cup.
- Vanilla extract, 2 tbsp.

Topping:

- 1/2 cup of all-purpose flour
- 1/2 cup of brown sugar, firmly packed.
- 1 tsp of cinnamon, ground.
- 1/4 tsp of salt.
- nutmeg, freshly grated.
- 1 stick of refrigerated chopped butter (extra for serving).
- To serve, warm pancake syrup.
- For serving, 1 cup of fresh blueberries

INSTRUCTION

1. For the French toast: Use butter to grease the baking pan. Slice or tear the bread into cubes, then spread it evenly in the pan. In a large basin, crack the eggs. Eggs, milk, cream, granulated sugar, brown sugar, and vanilla are all combined in a bowl. Pour over the bread evenly. Until used, carefully cover the pan and keep it in the refrigerator.

2. For the topping: In another bowl, combine the flour, brown sugar, cinnamon, salt, and a little nutmeg. Together, stir with a fork. With a pastry cutter, combine everything and stir until the mixture resembles small stones. Refrigerate in a resealable plastic bag.

3. Set the oven to 350 degrees Fahrenheit when you're ready to bake the dish. Place the dish back in the refrigerator and top with the topping. For a harder, crispier texture, bake for one hour or more. For a softer, more bread pudding-like texture, bake for 45 minutes.

4. Scoop out chunks one at a time. Blueberries are garnished on top along with warm pancake syrup and butter.

APRICOT AMARETTO JAM

Prep Time: 30 min.

Process: 10 min.

Makes: 8 half-pints

INGREDIENTS

- 4-1/4 cups of crushed, peeled apricots, around 2 1/2 pounds.
- 1/4 cup of lemon juice.
- 6-1/4 cups of divided sugar.
- 1 package (1.3/4 oz) of fruit pectin powder.
- 1/2 tsp of unsalted butter.
- 1/3 cup of amaretto.

INSTRUCTION

1. Combine apricots and lemon juice in a Dutch oven. 1/4 cup pectin and sugar are combined in a small bowl and added to the apricot mixture. Add butter, if desired. Over medium-high heat, bring to a full rolling boil while stirring continuously. Stir in the remaining sugar gradually. Return to a full rolling boil and cook for 1 minute while stirring continuously.

2. Stir in amaretto after removing from heat. 5 minutes of jam cooling in a Dutch oven while stirring occasionally. With a 1/4-inch headspace, ladle the heated mixture into eight hot, sterilized half-pint jars. the rims. Center the lids on the jars and tighten the bands with a fingertip.

3. Make sure the jars are thoroughly submerged in water before placing them in the canner with simmering water. 10 minutes of processing after bringing to a boil Cool the jars after removal.

CHAPTER 2: SIDES & SALAD

CONSERVE PLUM

Total time: 50 minutes

Makes: 7 half-pints

INGREDIENTS

- 2 lbs. of medium Italian plums, pitted and quartered
- 1-1/2 cups of cranberries, dried
- 1/2 cup of mandarin oranges, quartered and thinly sliced
- 1/2 cup of orange juice
- 3 cups of sugar, divided
- 1 package (1-3/4 oz.) of powdered fruit pectin
- 1 cup of walnuts, coarsely chopped

INSTRUCTION

1. Combine plums, cranberries, oranges, orange juice, and 2-1/2 cups sugar in a Dutch oven. Mix pectin and the remaining sugar; reserve. Over high heat, bring to a full rolling boil while stirring continuously for about 15 minutes, or until somewhat thickened and the plums soften. Add walnuts and pectin mixture; stir to a high rolling boil again. Stir and boil for one minute.

2. Get rid of the heat. Fill 7 heated half-pint jars with the hot mixture, leaving a 1/4-inch headspace. By adding hot mixture, remove air bubbles and, if necessary, adjust headspace. the rims. Center the lids on the jars and tighten the bands with a fingertip.

3. Make sure the jars are thoroughly submerged in water before placing them in the canner with simmering water. 10 minutes of processing after bringing to a boil Cool the jars after removal.

SOFT BEER PRETZEL NUGGETS

Total Time

Prep: 1 hour

rising Bake: 10 min./batch

Makes: 8 dozen

INGREDIENTS

- 1 bottle (12 oz.) of amber beer (or nonalcoholic beer)
- 1 package of active dry yeast
- 2 tbsp. of unsalted melted butter
- 2 tbsp. of sugar
- 1-1/2 tsp. salt
- 4-1/2 cups of all-purpose flour
- 10 cups of water
- 2/3 cup of baking soda

topping

- 1 large egg yolk
- 1 tbsp. water
- Coarse salt

INSTRUCTION

1. Heat the beer to between 110° and 115° in a small saucepan, then turn off the heat. Add yeast and stir until dissolved. Combine the yeast mixture, butter, sugar, salt, and 3 cups of flour in a large bowl. Beat on medium speed until smooth. Add just enough of the remaining flour to stir a soft dough (dough will be sticky).
2. Turn dough onto a floured surface and knead for 6 to 8 minutes, or until it is elastic and smooth. Place in a greased bowl after giving the top a quick flip. Cover and allow to rise until doubled, about an hour, in a warm location.
3. the oven to 425 degrees. Put down the dough. Turn out onto a surface that has been lightly dusted with flour; divide into 8 balls. Create a 12-inch rope out of each. Give each rope a 1-inch cut.

4. Bring 10 cups of water and baking soda to a boil in a Dutch oven. 12 at a time, drop the nuggets into the hot water. For 30 seconds, cook. Remove with a slotted spoon, then thoroughly dry with paper towels.
5. Put on oiled baking trays. Brush pretzels with an egg yolk mixture made with 1 tablespoon water in a small bowl. If desired, sprinkle some coarse salt. Bake for 10 to 12 minutes, or until golden. Remove from pans and cool on a wire rack.

GERMAN POTATO DUMPLINGS

Total Time

Prep: 40 min. Cook: 10 min.

Makes

8 servings

INGREDIENTS

- 3 lbs. of medium potatoes, peeled
- 1 cup of all-purpose flour
- 3 large eggs
- 2/3 cup of bread crumbs, dried
- 1 tsp salt
- 1/2 tsp ground nutmeg
- 12 cups of water

browned butter sauce:

- 1/2 cup of cubed butter
- 1 tbsp. onion, chopped
- 1/4 cup bread crumbs, dried

INSTRUCTION

1. In a Dutch oven, pour water to cover the potatoes. up to a boil. Reduce heat; cook for 15-20 minutes, uncovered, or until fork-tender. Transfer to a large bowl after draining.
2. Make potato mash. Stir bread crumbs, salt, nutmeg, flour, and eggs. Into sixteen (2-inch) balls, form.
3. Bring 12 cups of water to a boil in a Dutch oven. Add the dumplings slowly. When a toothpick is placed in the center of a dumpling, it should come out clean after 7-9 minutes of simmering, so lower the heat.
4. In the meantime, melt butter and onion in a small, heavy saucepan over medium heat. Stirring continuously, heat for 5-7 minutes or until butter is golden brown. Stir bread crumbs after removing from the heat. Offer dumplings alongside.

MEXICAN FIESTA PLATTER

Total Time

Prep: 15 min. Cook: 35 min.

Makes 20 servings

INGREDIENTS

- 2-1/2 of lbs. of ground beef
- 2 cans (each 16 oz.) rinsed and drained kidney beans
- 2 cans (each 15 oz.) of tomato sauce
- 1 envelope of chili seasoning
- 1 package (9-1/4 oz.) of corn chips
- 3 cups of hot cooked rice
- 2 large chopped onions
- 2 cups of Monterey Jack cheese, shredded
- 1 shredded medium head iceberg lettuce
- 4 chopped medium tomatoes,
- 1-1/2 cups of ripe olives, chopped
- Hot pepper sauce

INSTRUCTION

1. Cook the beef in a Dutch oven over medium heat for 5 to 7 minutes, or until it is no longer pink. Crumble the steak and drain. Stir occasionally while simmering the beans, tomato sauce, and chili seasoning for 30 minutes.
2. Place the corn chips, rice, onions, meat mixture, cheese, lettuce, tomato, and olives on 2 serving dishes with sides. If desired, sprinkle a little spicy sauce.

WARM FARRO AND ROASTED BUTTERNUT SQUASH SALAD

Prep Time: 15 Minutes

Cook Time: 30 Minutes

Servings: 4 Servings

INGREDIENTS

- 2 tablespoon Olive oil
- 1 diced shallot
- 1 cup of Farro
- 1 quart of Vegetable broth
- 1 bunch of Kale stemmed, finely chopped
- 2 tablespoons of lemon juice
- 1/4 cup of Olive oil
- 1 tablespoon of Dijon mustard
- 1 Butternut Squash, Diced and roasted
- 1/2 cup of Feta or ricotta
- Salt and pepper as needed

INSTRUCTIONS

1. The shallots should be sweated for one to two minutes over medium heat in a large saucepot (we like to use a Dutch oven for this).
2. Add the farro and a large pinch of salt after deglazing the pan with the stock.
3. Bring to a simmer, reduce heat, and then cover the saucepan.
4. For thirty minutes, cook the grains.
5. Make your dressing by combining the lemon juice, mustard, and salt in a large bowl while the farro is heating.
6. Add the olive oil gradually before tossing the greens with the dressing.
7. If necessary, drain the warm farro before adding it to the dressing and tossing.

8. Add the squash (and cheese, if desired).

BEST CHICKEN SALAD

Servings: 4

INGREDIENTS

- 4 lbs. of bone-in, skin-on chicken breasts
- 2 scallions, cut
- ¼ tsp. of black peppercorns
- ½ tsp of Dijon mustard
- 3 pale green celery ribs, diced
- ½ cup of onion, minced
- ½ cup of walnut or pecan halves
- 1 halved lemon
- ⅔ cup of mayonnaise
- ¼ cup of sour cream to taste
- 3 tbsp of chopped fresh parsley, tarragon or chives
- Salt and ground black pepper as needed

INSTRUCTION

1. Select a Dutch oven or heavy pot with a tight-fitting lid. It should be just large enough to tightly fit the chicken within. Do not add the chicken to the pot until it is roughly two-thirds full of cold water. Tea kettle with additional water on the stove.

2. Add peppercorns and scallions to the water, cover, and bring to a boil. Put chicken pieces into the heated water after turning off the heat. If more water is required to cover the chicken by 2 inches, add it from the kettle. Put the lid back on and let the chicken soak for about 2 hours in the boiling water. Do not restart the flame; the pot will continue to heat up sufficiently to cook the chicken properly and safely. (To perform the test, split a piece of chicken in half and examine the meat around the bone. If it's still pink, put the pot back on low heat, bring the water to a simmer, and let it cook for an additional 10 minutes.)

3. Remove the chicken from the pot. Remove and discard the skin, fat, and bones. With paper towels, pat the meat dry before slicing or shredding it into bite-sized pieces and

placing it in a bowl. (Also, simmer the cooking liquid until it is flavorful, strain it, and then store it in the fridge or freezer to use as chicken stock.)

4. Combine 1/2 lemon juice, mayonnaise, and sour cream in a bowl. Add mustard or brine, if using, by whisking. To your liking, taste and adjust the thickness and seasonings. Pour over the chicken and use a rubber spatula to thoroughly wipe the bowl.

5. Add salt, pepper, nuts, herbs, celery, and, if using, onion. Gently but completely toss. For at least 4 hours, refrigerate covered. If necessary, taste and add salt and pepper. Before serving, sprinkle with herbs.

SPICED PEAR RISOTTO

Total Time

Prep: 15 min. Cook: 35 min.

Servings: 10

INGREDIENTS

- 6 cups of chicken broth
- 1/2 cup of sweet onion, finely chopped
- 1/2 cup of sweet red pepper, finely chopped
- 1 minced garlic clove
- 3 tbsp. butter
- 3 cups of uncooked arborio rice
- 1/2 tsp. Chinese five-spice powder
- Dash cayenne pepper
- 1/4 cup of apple cider or juice
- 1 large pear, peeled and chopped
- 1/2 cup of grated Parmesan cheese, divided
- 1/2 tsp coarsely ground pepper
- Chopped chives

INSTRUCTION

1. Heat the broth in a large pot, then keep it warm. In a Dutch oven, saute the onion, red pepper, and garlic in butter for 3 minutes or until they are soft.
2. Cook and stir for two to three minutes after adding the rice, cayenne, and five-spice powder. Add cider and lower the heat to medium. Until all of the liquid has been absorbed, cook and stir.
3. Stirring continuously, add 1/2 cup at a time of warm broth. The liquid should have time to absorb between additions. Just until the rice is almost soft and the risotto is creamy. (Approximately 25 minutes of cooking time.)
4. Cook and stir until cooked through after adding the pear, 1/4 cup cheese, and pepper. Sprinkle the remaining cheese over top. Top with minced chives if preferred.

CLASSIC RED BEANS AND RICE

Total Time

Prep Time: 10 min.

Cook Time: 2-1/4 hours & standing

 Servings: 8

INGREDIENTS

- 1 lb. kidney beans, dried
- 8 cups of water
- 1 ham hock
- 2 bay leaves
- 1 tsp. onion powder
- 1 lb. ground beef
- 1 chopped large onion
- 1 tsp. salt
- 1/2 tsp. pepper
- 1 minced garlic clove
- Hot cooked rice
- fresh parsley, Chopped

INSTRUCTION

1. After sorting, rinse the beans in cold water. In a Dutch oven, add the beans and 2 inches of water to cover them. Boil for 2 minutes after bringing to a boil. Take the pot off the heat, cover it, and let the beans sit for 1-4 hours to soften.
2. The liquid from the beans is drained and rinsed away. Go back to the Dutch oven. Add the ham hock, bay leaves, onion powder, and 8 cups of water. up to a boil. Simmer for an hour on low heat with a cover.
3. Cook the beef, onion, salt, and pepper over medium heat in a large cast-iron or other heavy skillet until the meat is no longer pink. Crumble the beef. For an additional minute, add the garlic. Drain. the bean mixture with. 1 hour of uncovered simmering Remove the bay leaves.

4. Take out the ham hock and let it cool. Separate the meat off the bone and discard it. Return meat to broth after cutting into bite-sized pieces. Warm thru. If preferred, garnish with finely chopped fresh parsley and serve with rice.

CREAMY MUSHROOMS

Total Time

Prep/Total Time: 25 min.

Makes

8 servings

INGREDIENTS

- 3 lbs. fresh mushrooms, sliced
- 1/2 cup of butter, cubed
- 1/2 cup of all-purpose flour
- 2-1/2 cups of whole milk
- 1 cup of evaporated milk
- 2 tsp salt

INSTRUCTION

1. In a large stockpot, add the mushrooms and cover with water. Stir and bring to a boil. Reduce heat, cover, and simmer for 3 minutes or until fork-tender. Good drainage
2. Melt butter inside a Dutch oven. As you gradually add the milk and evaporated milk, stir in the flour until it's smooth. Bring to a boil; simmer and stir for 2 minutes or until thickened. Add salt and mushrooms and stir. Cook and stir for 3 to 4 minutes over medium heat until thoroughly cooked.

BUFFALO STYLE CAULIFLOWER

Prep time: 15 minutes

Cooking time: 25 minutes

Servings: 4

INGREDIENTS:

- 2 tablespoon olive oil
- 1 head cauliflower
- Salt and pepper as needed
- 2 tablespoons of unsalted butter
- ¼ cup of red-hot sauce
- 1 tablespoon of fresh lime juice
- parsley or cilantro, Chopped

INSTRUCTIONS:

1. Turn on the 375°F oven.
2. Cut away the tough bloom portion near the cauliflower's base. Small to medium-sized florets should be broken off.
3. Melt butter in a microwave-safe bowl.
4. Stir in lime juice and spicy sauce to butter.
5. Heat a Dutch oven over a medium flame.
6. Flake cauliflower and oil to the pan. For 4-5 minutes, saute until beautifully browned.
7. Stir the spicy sauce mixture after adding it, then pour it in.
8. Bake cauliflower for 15 to 20 minutes, or until tender.
9. Sprinkle cilantro or parsley after taking the oven racks out.

BUTTERMILK BISCUITS

Prep time: 20 minutes

Cook time: 15 minutes

Servings: 10

INGREDIENTS

- 1 cup of all-purpose flour
- 1 cup of whole wheat flour
- 2 tbsp. sugar
- 4 tsp. of baking powder
- ¼ tsp of baking soda
- ¼ tsp salt
- 4 tbsp. butter, softened
- 1¼ cups of cold buttermilk

INSTRUCTIONS

1. Set the oven to 400 °F.
2. Combine the flours, sugar, baking soda, baking powder, and salt in a bowl.
3. Add the softened butter and stir with your fingertips until the flour mixture resembles coarse crumbs.
4. Forming a soft dough, stir in the buttermilk.
5. On a floured surface, place the dough and pat it into a circle that is 34 inch thick.
6. Cut out biscuits with a 2-inch biscuit cutter, collecting dough as necessary to form additional biscuits.
7. Place biscuits in Dutch oven and bake for 12 minutes or until golden brown.

CRUNCHY PARMESAN AND GARLIC ZUCCHINI

Prep time: 15 minutes

Cook time: 20 minutes

Servings: 4

INGREDIENTS

- 3 tablespoon of olive oil
- 4-6 small green zucchini, sliced
- Coarse salt and pepper as needed
- 4 garlic cloves, thinly sliced
- 1 cup of panko crumbs
- 1 cup of freshly grated parmesan

INSTRUCTIONS

1. set the oven to 450 degrees.
2. Medium-low heat is used to warm the oil in a large Dutch oven.
3. Add the zucchini and cook for 3 minutes on one side before turning. 3 more minutes of cooking.
4. Sprinkle salt and pepper to taste.
5. Add the garlic slices, and cook for one minute.
6. Top with grated cheese and panko crumbs.
7. Transfer to oven and bake for 5 to 10 minutes, or until brown and bubbling.

PANCETTA AND ASPARAGUS WITH FRIED EGG

Prep time: 15 minutes

Cooking time: 10 minutes

Servings: 4

INGREDIENTS:

- 1 tablespoon olive oil
- ¼ lb. pancetta
- 3 small shallots, thinly sliced
- ½ lb. asparagus
- Salt and pepper as needed
- 2 eggs

INSTRUCTIONS

1. Dutch oven with olive oil on heat.
2. Stirring frequently when frying the pancetta Place on a platter.
3. Shallots are added and cooked for 2 minutes.
4. Saute the asparagus pieces for a while after adding them.
5. Sprinkle with salt and pepper, then keep an eye out to make sure the asparagus is thoroughly cooked and browned.
6. Re-add the pancetta and stir everything together. Place on a platter.
7. Fry an egg in the pan, using additional oil if required.
8. Add salt and pepper and a fried egg to the mixture of asparagus and pancetta.

CHAPTER 3: DESSERTS

DUTCH OVEN APPLE COBBLER

Prep Time: 10 minutes

Cook Time: 20 minutes

Total Time: 30 minutes

INGREDIENT

- 1.5 lbs. sliced apples
- ¼ cup granulated sugar
- 1 tbsp. cinnamon
- 1 cup of flour
- ¼ cup of granulated sugar
- 1 tsp. baking powder
- 1 tsp. cinnamon
- 1/4 tsp. salt
- ¼ cup of cold butter, cold
- 1/3 cup of milk

INSTRUCTIONS

1. A 10" (4 quart) Dutch oven should be lined with parchment paper and 21 coals prepared.
2. CONDUCT THE FILLING: Apples should be cored and sliced. Sprinkle 1 tablespoon of cinnamon and 1/4 cup of sugar over them before placing them in the Dutch oven. Cinnamon and sugar on the apples and stir to combine.
3. In a mixing bowl, combine the dry ingredients (flour, baking powder, 1/4 cup sugar, 1 tsp cinnamon, salt). Add the butter to the bowl after cutting it into small pieces. Rub the butter into the dry ingredients with your fingers until a crumbly meal forms. To combine a dough, add the milk and gently mash together.
4. Slice off pieces of dough, then scatter them over the apples. Instead of having one large glob of dough in the middle, you want small pockets of dough distributed equally.

5. Set the Dutch oven's lid in order to bake the Cobbler. Set the Dutch oven on a ring of seven coals, and then place 14 coals, spaced equally, on top of the cover to produce the same amount of heat as a 350°F oven. Bake the topping for 30 to 40 minutes, or until golden brown.
6. Serve after removing from heat!

DUTCH OVEN UPSIDE DOWN PEACH CAKE

Prep Time: 15 Minutes

Cook Time: 15 Minutes

Total Time: 30 Minutes

INGREDIENTS

- 1/2 cup of softened butter
- 1/4 cup of Canola or vegetable oil
- 3/4 cup of brown sugar
- 1 cup of sugar
- 3 eggs
- 2 cups of all-purpose flour
- 1 tsp. baking soda
- 1 tsp. baking powder
- 1 tsp. salt
- 1 tsp. cinnamon
- 1 cup of buttermilk
- 1/4 cup of butter
- 1/2 cup of brown sugar
- 4 peeled and sliced peaches

INSTRUCTIONS

1. Approximately one hour before serving:
2. A 12-inch Dutch oven should be cleaned and lightly sprayed with cooking oil inside before use.
3. 25 coals should be heated for cooking (the recipe calls for 19, but I always heat up extras). It will take about 30 minutes to complete this. Prepare the cake while the coals are warming up. When ready, the coals will turn white.
4. In a bowl, combine butter, oil, and sugars. until smooth, beat.
5. Add the eggs and beat for approximately a minute, or until creamy and fluffy.

6. Add the cinnamon, salt, soda, powder, and flour. Pulse the ingredients together thoroughly until the flour is completely dissolved.

7. The buttermilk should be added to the batter in the bowl one small amount at a time while the mixer is still running on low. Mix sure all the ingredients are combined by mixing for an additional minute.

8. Butter should be melted in the Dutch oven's bottom to create the foundation layer. In the bottom of the Dutch oven, put the peaches in a single layer after adding the brown sugar.

9. Place the lid on top of the Dutch oven and pour the cake mix over the peaches.

10. Place 7 hot coals underneath the Dutch oven and 12 hot coals on top of it.

11. Set a 12-minute timer. Cooking the cake will take 10 to 15 minutes. Remove the cake after 12 minutes of baking so that the Dutch Oven is not placed over the embers. Continue baking for a further few minutes, often 3–4, with coals on top. To test the cake, place a toothpick in the center. The cake is finished when a toothpick put in the center comes out clean.

12. Serve with vanilla ice cream or whipped cream.

DUTCH OVEN BROWNIES

Prep Time: 5 Minutes

Cook Time: 45 Minutes

Extra Time: 15 Minutes

Total Time: 1 hr. 5 Minutes

Servings: 12 Serving

INGREDIENTS

- 1 18.3 ounces box of brownie mix
- 1 can dark soda pop
- 12 ounces bag of chocolate chips

INSTRUCTIONS

1. For the Dutch oven, prepare the charcoal.
2. The Dutch oven should have a liner in it.
3. Mix soda and the brownie mix.
4. Bake the batter in the oven.
5. The middle of the batter should contain the bag of chocolate chips.
6. Bake for around 30 to 60 minutes.

Note

o   Reduce the soda if you are worried that the mix will be excessively liquidy.

CHOCOLATE RASPBERRY COBBLER

Total Time: 50 Minutes

4 Servings

INGREDIENTS

- Nonstick cooking spray
- 1 can (21 oz.) raspberry pie filling
- 1 pouch (1.1½-lbs) double chocolate chunk, cookie mix
- 3/4 of melted Butter

INSTRUCTION

1. Get ready to cook over your campfire.
2. Prepare 28–30 coals for when you're prepared to start cooking. Using nonstick cooking spray, line a 10-in (25.4-cm) Dutch oven with parchment paper. The Dutch oven's bottom needs 10 coals, and the lid needs 18 to 20. After 30 minutes of baking, the coals might need to be refilled. The ideal baking temperature is 350°F (177°C).
3. In your prepared Dutch oven, spread the raspberry pie filling evenly throughout the bottom.
4. Over the filling, strew the chocolate chunk cookie mix.
5. Spread the cookie mix with a spoon after pouring the melted butter over it evenly.
6. The topping should be set after about 30 minutes of baking the cobbler.
7. Before serving, let aside to chill for 10 to 15 minutes.
8. Enjoy.

DUTCH BABY WITH BERRIES

Cook Time: 45 Minutes

6 Servings

INGREDIENTS

- 9 eggs
- 1 1/2 cups of Whole milk
- 1 tbsp. Vanilla extract
- Zest of 1 lemon
- 1 1/2 cups of Flour
- 1/2 tsp. Salt
- 1/2 cup pf Butter
- 4 cups of Berries, of choice
- 1/4 cup of Confectioner's sugar
- For serve freshly squeezed lemon juice

INSTRUCTION

1. Get ready to cook over your campfire.
2. Prepare a 12-in (30.5-cm) Dutch oven when you're ready to start cooking. The top of the Dutch oven lid needs 14 coals, and the area around it needs 7 coals. After 30 minutes of baking, the coals might need to be refilled.
3. Combine the milk, lemon zest, vanilla extract, and eggs in a bowl. When you're ready to cook the Dutch Baby, stir the salt and flour together until well-combined.
4. Put 8 coals under the Dutch oven after the coals are nice and hot. Melt a cube of butter by adding it to the pan. Add the batter once it has melted, then cover with a lid. 16 coals should be placed atop the lid.
5. Cook until set, about 25 minutes, rotating the lid 1/4 turn every 5 minutes. When the lid is removed, it will deflate after puffing up to the top of the lid.
6. Take the Dutch oven from the stove.

7. Add berries, confectioner's sugar, and a squeeze of fresh lemon juice before covering. Recover the Dutch oven's lid, then reheat the berries before serving.
8. Slice into 6 pieces, then devour.

CINNAMON RICE PUDDING

Prep time: 15 minutes

Cook time: 50 minutes

Servings: 6

INGREDIENTS

- 1 tablespoon butter
- 2 cups of cooked white rice
- ½ teaspoon ground cinnamon
- 3/4 cup of sugar
- 5 large eggs
- 2 cups of heavy cream
- 1 teaspoon vanilla extract
- For garnish sprinkle of ground cinnamon

INSTRUCTIONS

1. the oven to 350 degrees Fahrenheit.
2. Rice is added to a 2-quart Dutch oven that has been buttery inside.
3. Mix the eggs, sugar, and cinnamon thoroughly in a large bowl.
4. Add the cream and vanilla by whisking.
5. Gently pour the mixture over the rice. Place the Dutch oven in the oven and cover with the lid. The custard must bake for 50 minutes or until it is set. After taking it out of the oven, sprinkle it liberally with cinnamon.
6. Serve hot.

RHUBARB & STRAWBERRY CRISP

Prep Time: 20 Minutes

Cook Time: 35 To 40 Minutes

Servings: 7

INGREDIENT

- 6 tbsp. butter
- 3 cups of sliced rhubarb
- 3 cups of sliced strawberries
- 3/4 cup sugar
- 1 tbsp. cornstarch
- 3/4 cup of flour
- 3/4 cup of brown sugar
- 1/2 cup of rolled oats
- 1/2 tsp. cinnamon

INSTRUCTION

1. set the oven to 350 degrees Fahrenheit.
2. A Dutch oven should be butter-greased.
3. Combine the rhubarb, strawberries, sugar, and cornstarch in a large bowl. In the Dutch oven, put the fruit mixture.
4. Use two forks to combine the flour, brown sugar, and remaining 6 tablespoons of butter together until the mixture resembles coarse crumbs. Add the cinnamon and oats.
5. Mix once more. Spoon a topping on top of the fruit mixture.
6. For 35 to 40 minutes, or until the top is slightly browned and crisp, bake the pot covered.

NOTE

- Rhubarb is one of the least sprayed or treated crops due to its high level of disease resistance, making conventionally cultivated rhubarb nearly identical to organic. When purchasing rhubarb, make sure the stalks' two ends are not dried out. Use within a few days if refrigerated; otherwise, freeze.

CHOCOLATE BREAD PUDDING

Prep Time: 20 Minutes

Cook Time: 1 To 1 1/4 Hours

Servings: 5

INGREDIENT

- For greasing Butter
- 8 cups of sweet bread, cut into cubes melted unsalted butter
- 1 cup of sugar
- 1/2 cup of cocoa powder
- 2 tsp. cinnamon
- 1 tsp. vanilla extract
- 1/2 tsp. almond extract
- 1/4 teaspoon salt
- 3 cups whole milk
- 4 large eggs
- 1/2 cup chocolate chips, divided

INSTRUCTION

1. the oven to 350 degrees Fahrenheit.
2. Butter should be used liberally to coat a Dutch oven.
3. Place the bread pieces in the Dutch oven after tossing in the melted butter. Until lightly golden brown, bake for 8 to 10 minutes.
4. Combine the sugar, cocoa powder, cinnamon, vanilla, almond extract, and salt in a large bowl. Whisk in the milk and eggs after adding them. Bread cubes should be added and folded until uniformly wet. After the bread cubes have absorbed the majority of the liquid, let sit for 15 to 20 minutes, folding once or twice.
5. Refill the Dutch oven with half of the bread mixture. Sprinkle 1/4 cup of chocolate chips on top. Add the remaining bread mixture on top, followed by the last 1/4 cup of chocolate chips.

6. Bake for 1 to 1 1/4 hours, with the lid on, until the top puffs up and a knife inserted close to the center comes out mostly clean.

NOTES

- Drizzle dulce de leche on top to serve. Dulce de leche is a spread that is made from a mixture of milk and sugar that has been carefully heated until the sugars have caramelized and become thick, creamy, and strongly flavored. It is incredibly well-liked throughout Latin America and is now generally accessible here as well. You might even create your own! In your Dutch oven, add a 12-ounce can of condensed milk and stir continuously over medium-low heat until a cooled tablespoon can be turned upside-down without the dulce de leche dropping off.

BAKED APPLES WITH CARAMEL SAUCE

Prep Time: 15 Minutes

Cook Time: 25 Minutes

Servings: 6

INGREDIENT

- 8 tbsp. butter
- 6 apples, peeled and cored
- 1/2 cup of granulated sugar, divided
- 1 1/2 tsp. cinnamon
- 1 1/4 cups of brown sugar
- 3 tbsp. water

INSTRUCTION

1. The oven should be heated to 325°F.
2. 1 tablespoon of the butter should be used to coat a Dutch oven.
3. To produce a level surface, trim a tiny portion of each apple's bottom. Put the apples in the Dutch oven with the cut side facing out. Each apple should have one half of the remaining 3 tablespoons of butter on top of it.
4. Sprinkle the apples with the granulated sugar and cinnamon that you've combined in a small bowl. For 15 to 20 minutes, bake with the cover on until the sugar has melted. Place the apples in a serving bowl.
5. Combine the water, 8 more tablespoons of granulated sugar, and brown sugar to the Dutch oven. Stirring often, bring to a boil over medium heat, and simmer for about 5 minutes or until thick. Add the remaining butter and whisk. Over each apple, smear some caramel sauce.

CHAPTER 4: STEW AND SOUP

CHICKEN AND DUMPLINGS

Prep Time: 30 Minutes

Cook Time: 35 Minutes

Total Time: 1 Hour 5 Minutes

Servings: 5

INGREDIENTS

- 2 tablespoons of vegetable oil.
- 2 sizable breasts of chicken.
- Salt and pepper as needed.
- 1/3 cup of butter.
- 1 1/2 tsp minced garlic.
- 2 substantial celery stalks, chopped (around 1 cup)
- Diced 2 big carrots (around 1 cup)
- Cubed 8 tiny potatoes (about 1- 1 1/2 cups)
- Parsley, 1 tbsp
- ⅓ cup of butter.
- 1 ½ tsp minced garlic.
- 2 big celery stalks, chopped (around 1 cup)
- Diced 2 big carrots (around 1 cup)
- Cubed 8 tiny potatoes (about 1- 1 12 cups)
- 1 tbsp of parsley
- 1 tsp. of basil
- 1/2 tsp. thyme
- To taste, add salt and pepper.
- ¼ cup of all-purpose flour
- 8 cups of vegetable or chicken stock.
- 1 ½ cups of cream.

DUMPLINGS

- 2 cups of all-purpose flour
- 1 cup of your preferred milk.
- 2 tbsp of melted butter

- 2 tbsp of extra virgin olive oil.
- 1 tbsp baking powder
- 1 1/2 tsp of parsley
- 1/2 tsp. of basil
- 1/2 tsp. thyme
- 1/2 tsp of pepper.
- 1/4 teaspoon of salt

INSTRUCTIONS

To prepare the stew:

1. Put the chicken breast aside after liberally seasoning it with salt and pepper.
2. The vegetable oil should be added to a sizable heavy-bottomed pot or Dutch oven and heated over medium heat. To the hot oil, add the seasoned chicken breasts.
3. The chicken breasts should be cooked through with frequent flipping.
4. Shred the chicken breasts with two forks after transferring them to a plate. Place aside.
5. Melt the butter in the same pot over medium-low heat. To remove any stuck-on pieces, carefully scrape the pot's bottom. Add the minced garlic to the melted butter and cook for 30 seconds or until fragrant.
6. Add the salt, pepper, celery, carrots, potatoes, parsley, basil, and thyme. After combining, stir a tight-fitting lid to the pot. During the five minutes the vegetables are cooking, stir them occasionally.
7. Remove the lid five minutes later. The flour should be sprinkled on top of the veggies and mixed in thoroughly.
8. Shredded chicken, cream, and broth should all be added to the saucepan. The stew should first be heated to a rolling boil before being simmered. For 10 to 15 minutes, cover the stew and let it simmer.

To Make the Dumplings:

1. Combine the flour, milk, melted butter, olive oil, baking powder, parsley, basil, thyme, pepper, and salt in a medium-sized bowl. Using a strong wooden spoon, combine the ingredients to form a shaggy dough. Then, knead it for two to three minutes on a surface that has been lightly dusted with flour.

2. Roll dough into balls by pinching off bits the size of golf balls. Repetition is required to portion out and form balls out of all the dough.

Preparing The Dumplings:

1. When the timer goes off, take the lid off and give the stew a good stir.
2. Add the dumplings while the stew is still simmering. After adding the dumplings, DO NOT STIR THE Soup.
3. Set a 14-minute timer and replace the lid. During this period, don't lift the lid. It is essential to keep the lid on since the steam will cook the dumplings.
4. After the allotted time has passed, turn off the heat, take the lid off, and let the stew five minutes to rest before serving.

NOTES

- o   Cream: For this recipe, any kind of cream may be used. We tested this recipe using full-fat, table cream, half-and-half, and canned coconut milk; we advise using one of these four.
- o   Milk: If you'd prefer, you can substitute cream for the milk in the dumplings. These dumplings have been tried with canned coconut milk, ordinary 1 percent cows' milk, almond milk, and half and half.
- o   For up to three days, leftovers can be kept in the refrigerator in an airtight container.

GREEK LEMON CHICKEN SOUP WITH RICE

Prep Time: 30 Minutes

Cook Time: 30 Minutes

Total Time: 1 Hour

INGREDIENTS

- 1 chicken, 3 pounds.
- 1 medium onion, cut into quarters.
- Garlic, 3 cloves.
- 12 cups of water
- 2 tbsp. of paste from chicken bouillon.
- salt kosher.
- 3 large eggs
- 2 juiced lemons.
- 1 cup of Basmati rice.
- Black pepper, freshly cracked, for serving.
- For serving, use olive oil.

INSTRUCTIONS

1. Place the whole chicken, the onion, the garlic, and enough water to cover the chicken in a big pot. The water should be heated to a boil and then simmered. To get the meat to fall off the bone, simmer the chicken for two to three hours. Take the chicken out of the water when it is tender, then place it somewhere to cool. Use a fine-mesh strainer to pour the chicken stock into a large measuring cup or another pot. Put the stock back in the pot.

2. Bring the stock back to a boil by adding 4 cups of more water, bouillon paste, and a teaspoon of salt.

3. When the chicken is cold enough to handle, remove it from the bones while the stock mixture is rising to a boil. Eggs and lemon juice should also be combined, then set aside.

4. Rice and pulled chicken should be added once the chicken stock has reached a rolling boil. After 5 minutes of cooking, return the mixture to a simmer.
5. Temper the egg and lemon mixture while the rice is cooking by slowly adding a cup of the broth while whisking continuously (do not add too much hot stock at once or the eggs will become scrambled). For about 2 minutes, continuously stir the egg mixture into the simmering stock/chicken/rice mixture.
6. Cook the soup over low heat for about 5 minutes, stirring constantly, until it thickens and becomes velvety.
7. The soup should be taken off the stove and left to cool for 10 minutes so that it can gradually thicken.
8. Pour the soup into bowls and sprinkle with a little black pepper and olive oil.

HEALING CHICKEN NOODLE SOUP

Prep Time: 5 Mins

Cook Time: 25 Mins

Total Time: 30 Mins

Servings: 6

INGREDIENTS

- 1 tablespoon of olive oil.
- Peeled and sliced into 1/3-inch circles, 4 medium carrots.
- sliced and halved 3 celery stalks.
- Diced 1 medium onion
- 2 chopped garlic cloves.
- 1 teaspoon turmeric
- 1 teaspoon of fresh thyme leaves, or use 1/2 teaspoon dried thyme.
- 1 teaspoon chopped fresh rosemary, or use 1/2 teaspoon dried rosemary.
- 1/2 lemon juice and zest.
- 1.5 teaspoons of salt.
- Black pepper, 1/2 tsp.
- Cayenne pepper
- 1 leaf of bay.
- 8 cups of bone or chicken broth.
- 2–3 cups of dried egg noodles Although I love flat noodles, you can use any shape you like.
- 1 shredded and meat-free rotisserie chicken.
- 2-3 tablespoons freshly chopped parsley.
- pepper and salt to taste.

INSTRUCTIONS

1. Large Dutch oven or heavy pot with lid: Heat olive oil in pan over medium-high heat until hot and shimmering.

2. On medium heat, add the carrots, celery, and onion and cook for about 10 minutes, or until the vegetables are tender.

3. Add in the following: cayenne, salt, pepper, lemon zest, garlic, turmeric, thyme, and rosemary. Garlic should be aromatic after 1-2 minutes of sautéing over medium heat.

4. Add 1 bay leaf, 1/2 lemon's juice, and stream in chicken or bone broth. Over medium-high heat, stir everything together and bring to a boil.

5. Add 2-3 cups of egg noodles and the shredded chicken once the mixture comes to a boil. Bring to a boil once more, cover, and reduce heat to low.

6. The pasta should be tender after 10 to 15 minutes of simmering at low heat. Get rid of the heat. As desired, add more salt and pepper after tasting. Serve with parsley that has been chopped. Enjoy!

BEEF CABBAGE SOUP

Prep Time: 15 minutes

Cook Time: 45 minutes

Total Time: 1 hour 35 minutes

Servings: 9 cups

INGREDIENTS

- 1 pound of ground beef
- 1 medium head of chopped cabbage, equivalent to 4-5 cups.
- 1 diced red bell pepper
- 1 diced yellow onion
- 1 can of dark kidney beans, 16 oz.
- 2 sliced celery stalks.
- For the maximum flavor, I use 1 28-oz can of crushed tomatoes. I rough cut the tomatoes in the can while reserving the juice.
- 1 tsp of Worcestershire sauce.
- 1 teaspoon "better than bouillon" beef base that I prefer.
- 1 cup of beef broth
- 1/4 tsp of powdered garlic.
- To taste, add salt and pepper.
- octopus crackers

INSTRUCTIONS

1. Cook the ground beef in a sizable pot over medium heat, then drain.
2. To the beef, add the remaining ingredients. Add all of the ingredients, including the juice, to the tomatoes and beans. Bring to a boil and then simmer for about 30 minutes, or until the onion and celery are soft.
3. Serve it hot along with oyster crackers.

NOTES

Let it cool fully, then place it in an airtight container and freeze any leftovers. The soup can be stored for two to three months.

BROCCOLI SAUSAGE SOUP

Cook Time: 25 Mins

Total Time: 25 Mins

Servings: 4

INGREDIENTS:

- 1 tbsp of salted butter.
- 1 pound of mild bulk Italian sausage meat that has been cut into bite-sized pieces.
- 1 small onion, chopped
- 2 diced celery ribs
- Peeled and chopped or pressed using a garlic press, 2 garlic cloves.
- smokey hot paprika, 1/2 tsp.
- 3 cups of chicken broth
- 1 cup of water.
- 2 cups of tiny broccoli florets.
- 1 tsp. of dried oregano
- 1/2 cups of heavy cream.
- 1/4 cup of parmesan cheese, grated.
- 1-2 drops liquid smoke.

INSTRUCTIONS:

1. Melt the butter in a Dutch oven-style pot with a thick bottom. Sausage should be thoroughly browned. Perform this step-in batches if the pot you're using can't fit all the meat in a single layer. Transfer the sausage to a plate covered in paper towels using a slotted spoon and set aside.

2. Remove all but 1 tsp of the grease from the pot using a spoon, then add the onion and celery and sauté for about 3 minutes, or until they begin to soften. Add the smoked paprika and garlic and stir.

3. Add water and chicken broth, cover, and simmer. Add the broccoli and the cooked meat; cover and boil for about 5 minutes, or until the broccoli is soft.
4. Add the Parmesan, cream, and oregano. To taste, add liquid smoke.

NOTES

- o Liquid smoke is an effective ingredient. I advise you to add 1 splash at first, taste the soup, and then add more as desired.

FARMER'S MARKET ITALIAN SAUSAGE-TORTELLINI SOUP

Prep Time: 13 Minutes

Cook Time: 40 Minutes

Total Time: 53 Minutes

Makes: 13 Cups

INGREDIENTS

- 2 tsp. of extra-virgin olive oil
- Sweet Italian turkey sausage, 12 oz.
- 1 1/2 cups of finely sliced yellow onions.
- 1 1/4 cups of finely chopped green pepper
- Carrots, peeled and sliced, 3/4 cup.
- minced garlic, 2 tsp.
- 46–47 ounces of sodium-reduced, fat-free beef broth.
- 1 15-ounce can of Italian herbs tomato sauce.
- 1 can of vegetable juice, 5.5 ounces.
- 2 and a half cups of chopped zucchini
- 2 tablespoons of Italian seasoning mix without salt.
- 19 oz of cheese tortellini that was frozen.
- 1 1/4 cups of diced, seeded tomatoes.
- 1 cup of baby spinach, chopped.
- kosher salt as needed.
- serving parmesan cheese.

INSTRUCTIONS

1. Olive oil should be heated in a large soup pot on a medium heat. Garlic, carrot, green pepper, onion, and sausage should be added. About 10 mins, or until the sausage is well cooked and no longer pink, stirring regularly to break up the meat. Drain if necessary.

2. Italian spice, tomato sauce, vegetable juice, and zucchini should all be added. For a constant simmer, lower the heat to low or medium-low, cover the pot, and let the food simmer for 15 minutes.

3. tomatoes and tortellini to the mix for a total of 10 more minutes, or until the tortellini are done, cover the pot and raise the heat as necessary to bring it back to a simmer.

4. Add the spinach after turning the heat off. To make the flavors stand out, taste and adjust the seasoning, adding kosher salt only as needed.

5. Serve immediately and, if wanted, pass parmesan around the table.

NOTES

o Most tortellini package instructions state that tortellini cooked from frozen in boiling water take only a few minutes to cook, but since we are gently simmering them instead of bringing them to a full, rolling boil, we give them a little more time to cook and blend with the flavors of the soup. When serving, we prefer them to be fully cooked and still have some bite to them—not mushy and overcooked.

o The whole-wheat tortellini sold in our local stores is noticeably higher in fat, and we usually strive to balance our preference for whole-grain items against fat content and other nutritional considerations. As mentioned in the paragraph above, we also advise buying whole-grain pasta whenever possible. Just make an effort to select the healthiest tortellini you can. The amount of fat in different brands varies significantly, so be sure to carefully check the labels.

o The sodium concentration and spices in the specific brands and goods you buy can affect how much salt you need to add at the end, as was covered in more detail in the post. We typically find that we need to add around 1 teaspoon of salt at the very end of cooking, but we advise starting with less and a little at a time until the flavors of this soup are truly strong and rich. You might need a little less salt if you're topping this soup with salty parmesan cheese.

MEDITERRANEAN FISH STEW

Prep Time: 5 Minutes

Cook Time: 35 Minutes

Total Time: 40 Minutes

Servings: 4

INGREDIENTS

- 1 tbsp of olive oil.
- 1 diced onion
- 4 minced garlic cloves.
- 1 chopped fennel bulb.
- 1 diced red pepper.
- 1 glass of dry white wine.
- 1 can of diced tomatoes in juices, measuring 28 oz.
- 1 tsp crushed red pepper.
- 1 tsp. dried oregano
- Halibut, cod, or another firm white fish weighing 1 pound.
- 1/2 cup of freshly chopped herbs.
- 1/2 cup of feta crumbles.

INSTRUCTIONS

1. Over medium heat warms the olive oil in a big Dutch oven or pot with a heavy bottom. About 6 minutes of sautéing should soften the onion. Add the garlic and continue to sauté for another minute. Fennel and red peppers should be added and cooked only till tender.

2. White wine should be added and simmered for a few minutes, or until it has reduced by around half.

3. Add tomatoes, oregano, and red pepper flakes by stirring. For 15 to 20 minutes, cover and simmer. Use salt and pepper to taste to season. Depending on how much liquid simmered off, add a further half cup of water if necessary.
4. Add the fish after cutting it into bite-sized pieces. Continue to simmer for 5 minutes or until fish is well done.
5. Add the fresh herbs after turning the heat off. Place fresh feta on top after ladling the soup into cups.

NOTES

Use a firm white fish, such as grouper, halibut, cod, catfish, snapper, or monkfish.

Follow the recipe but stop before adding the fish to make the soup base a day ahead of time. The soup should be cooled and refrigerated before being heated up to a simmer and adding the fish just before serving.

QUICK DUTCH OVEN CHICKEN NOODLE SOUP

Prep Time: 10 mins

Cook Time: 25 mins

Total Time: 35 mins

Servings: 6

INGREDIENTS

- 1 tablespoon of olive oil
- 1 cup diced onion
- sliced carrots, 8 oz (5 large carrots)
- 2 oz. diced celery (2 ribs)
- 1 1/2 tbsp chicken bouillon in granules
- 3/4 tsp dried thyme
- 3/4 teaspoon dried parsley
- 1/2 teaspoon black pepper
- 10 cups of water
- 8 ounces of egg noodles,
- 1 bay leaf
- 4 cups diced, chopped, diced, or shredded cooked chicken
- 2 tbsp. chopped fresh parsley

INSTRUCTIONS

1. The Dutch oven is warmed up on a medium-high flame.
2. Add the oil once it's heated.
3. Add the onions and simmer, stirring often, for 1 minute.
4. Stirring frequently, add the carrots and celery; simmer for an additional two to three minutes, or until they start to soften.
5. Add the granulated bouillon, thyme, parsley, and pepper, and mix everything together until it blooms.

6. When the spices are fragrant, add the water and bay leaf and whisk to incorporate any herbs that may have adhered to the vegetables.
7. See the notes below if you're using rotisserie chicken from the shop.
8. Bring to a boil, then simmer for 5 minutes to let the liquid gradually decrease.
9. Taste for seasonings and adjust as necessary based on preferences.
10. Egg noodles should be added and cooked for the specified amount of time, stirring occasionally.
11. Add the chicken and toss thoroughly during the final minute of boiling the noodles.
12. Take the noodles off the heat when they are finished.
13. Add some fresh parsley as a garnish before serving.

NOTES

- substituting granulated bouillon for cubes.
- Replace the granulated chicken bouillon with 4-6 chicken bouillon cubes. Start with less, let it dissolve, then gradually add more as necessary.
- replacing water and chicken bouillon with broth.
- Start with 1/2 tsp of salt and add more salt until the desired flavor is achieved when using 10 cups of chicken broth. Even though the broth made without bouillon will have a less robust flavor, it will still be excellent.
- using a rotisserie chicken from the supermarket.
- Add all the renderings to the bottom of the container if you're buying rotisserie chicken from the grocery store. Then, to remove any leftover renderings, rinse the container out into the soup using the water for the soup. The best solution for this is hot water or broth.

THAI COCONUT SOUP

Prep Time: 15 minutes

Cook Time: 45 minutes

Total Time: 1 hour

INGREDIENTS

- Coconut oil, 1 tablespoon.
- 1/2 of a sliced onion.
- 2 chopped garlic cloves.
- 1/2 of a red jalapeno pepper, sliced, or a couple Thai chiles, halved.
- 3 1/4-inch pieces of ginger or galangal.
- 1 stalk of lemongrass, pounded with the side of a knife and cut into 2-inch-long pieces.
- Red Thai curry paste, 2 tsp.
- 4 cups chicken broth; if vegetarian or on Whole30, see Notes.
- 4 cups coconut milk or cream from a can, as noted in the notes.
- 2 medium chicken breasts, chopped into bite-sized pieces; see Notes for vegan/vegetarian options or to use shrimp.
- 8 ounces of thinly sliced white mushrooms.
- If on Whole30, add 1-2 tbsp. of coconut sugar; see notes.
- 1 1/2 to 2 tablespoons of fish sauce, plus additional amounts to taste; see Notes if on Whole30 or vegan
- 2 to 3 tbsp of lime juice.
- 2 to 3 thinly sliced green onions.
- For garnish, finely cut fresh cilantro.

INSTRUCTIONS

1. The coconut oil is heated in a medium saucepan over medium heat. For five minutes, or until the onions are softened, add the onion, garlic, jalapeno or chile, galangal or ginger, lemongrass, and red curry paste. Stir continuously. Bring to a boil after adding chicken broth. 30 minutes of simmering at low heat with the lid off.

2. Remove and discard the aromatics, which include the garlic, onions, lemongrass, and ginger. Add chicken breast, mushrooms, and coconut cream or milk. Add fish sauce, coconut aminos, and lime juice along with additional amounts of each flavoring to taste and simmer until chicken breast pieces are barely cooked through.
3. Cook for 2 minutes, then ladle into serving dishes and garnish with fresh cilantro and green onion slices.

NOTES

o Make sure to use coconut milk or cream. This recipe will not work with coconut lopez or coconut creamer since they are not the same as coconut cream or coconut milk.

o To substitute 1 pound of raw shrimp for the chicken, just stir it in. Simmer until the food is just done, pink, and transparent is gone.

o Build it Use Whole30-approved chicken broth. Instead of coconut sugar, use 2 teaspoons of coconut aminos. Use Red Boat fish sauce; it is the only brand of fish sauce that I have discovered to be acceptable.

o Make it vegetarian or vegan: Take use of vegetable stock, ideally an Asian kind. Use a 1-pound block of bite-sized cubes of firm or extra-firm tofu (regular or silken). Use soy sauce (to taste) in place of fish sauce for vegans.

CLASSIC MINESTRONE SOUP

Prep Time: 10 minutes

Cook Time: 20 minutes

Total Time: 30 minutes

Servings: 5

INGREDIENTS

- 1 cup of elbow macaroni or small shelled pasta.
- Vegetable broth in 6 cups.
- 2 tbsp. of red wine vinegar or dry wine.
- 1 cup of diced yellow onion.
- 3 minced garlic cloves
- 1/2 cup finely sliced celery stalks, cut in half.
- 1 cup thinly sliced, quartered carrots
- 1 cup of thinly sliced, halved zucchini.
- 14 ounces of diced tomatoes in a can.
- Kidney beans, 14 ounce can, drained.
- Great Northern beans, 14 ounce, drained can.
- 2 cups of roughly chopped packed baby spinach.
- 1 cup of chopped, frozen green beans.
- 1 tsp. dried basil
- 1 tsp. dried oregano
- Fresh sage, 1 tbsp.
- Olive oil extra virgin, 2 tbsp.
- To taste, coarse salt and ground black pepper.
- To garnish, use freshly chopped parsley.

INSTRUCTIONS

1. Olive oil is heated over medium-high heat in a big pot. Add zucchini, onion, carrot, celery, and other ingredients to the pot and stir-fry for 5 minutes, or until softened.

2. Add the oregano, basil, and garlic. Sauté until aromatic, for 30 to 1 minute.
3. Add wine and stir. Make sure to remove any burnt bits from the pan's bottom.
4. Add tomato sauce, beans, vegetable broth, and fresh sage. up to a boil. Reduce the heat to a simmer, stir the pasta, and cook for 9 to 10 minutes, stirring periodically, or until the pasta is al dente.
5. Add green beans and spinach. Cook green beans for 1-2 minutes, or until heated through. To taste, add salt and pepper. Add parsley as a garnish. Serve right away.

DUTCH OVEN CARROT GINGER SOUP

Prep Time: 10 MINS

Cook Time: 30 MINS

Total Time: 40 MINS

Servings: 6

INGREDIENTS

- Olive oil, 3 tbsp.
- 1 pound of chopped, peeled carrots.
- 1 wedged large yellow onion.
- 2 minced garlic cloves
- 1 1/2 tbsp of grated ginger.
- Pure maple syrup, 1 tbsp.
- 1 tsp dried thyme or 4 fresh sprigs.
- 2 dried bay leaves
- 1/2 tsp. ground dried sage.
- 1/2 tsp of salt.
- 1/4 tsp of nutmeg
- 1/4 a tsp of pepper.
- 2 to 4 cups of vegetable stock
- Optional heavy cream, 2/3 cup.

INSTRUCTIONS

1. On the stovetop, warm up the olive oil in a dutch oven over medium heat.
2. Before incorporating the onions, saute the carrots for 5 minutes. Carrots and onions should be sauteed for a further 10 minutes.
3. Put all the herbs and ingredients in the pot. Just a minute or two of cooking, with a few stirs.

4. Bring to a boil the vegetable stock after adding it. For 20 minutes, reduce to a simmer and cover.
5. Puree the soup after removing the bay leaves and thyme stalks.
6. Optional
7. Stir in the cream before adding fresh herbs like parsley or dill on top.

DUTCH OVEN BEEF STEW

Prep Time: 30 minutes

Cook Time: 2 hours 15 minutes

Total Time: 2 hours 45 minutes

Servings: 6 people

INGREDIENTS

For The Meat:

- 3 pounds of 1.5-inch chunks of entire, boneless beef chuck roast.
- Kosher salt, 1 1/2 tsp.
- 1 tsp of black pepper, ground.
- oil of olives

For The Stew:

- Diced 1 medium yellow onion.
- 5 minced garlic cloves
- Peeled and diced 3 big carrots.
- 1 tsp of finely chopped fresh thyme.
- Tomatoes paste, 2 tbsp.
- Worcestershire sauce, 2 tsp.
- 1/2 cup beef broth or red wine.
- 1/4 cup all-purpose flour, plus some additional amounts as needed.
- 4 cups of beef broth, plus more to taste.
- 3 peeled and diced medium Yukon gold potatoes - see note below.
- 2 bay leaves, dry.
- minced parsley
- Olive oil
- To taste, add salt and pepper.
- Green peas, fresh or frozen.

INSTRUCTIONS

1. Set the oven to 300 degrees Fahrenheit.
2. 1 1/2 tsp Kosher salt and 1 tsp freshly ground black pepper should be used to season meat chunks. Beef should be seared until well-browned on all sides in some olive oil over high heat in a big Dutch oven or heavy oven-proof saucepan. To avoid overcrowding the pan and to avoid overheating, do this in batches. If you see it starting to steam, drain the extra liquid and keep browning.
3. Browned meat should be moved to a platter and left aside. At this stage, it won't be entirely cooked. Don't wipe the pot clean; leave the brown pieces in place.
4. Using the same Dutch oven over medium heat, add some olive oil, onion, garlic, and carrots. Cook for about 5 minutes, stirring regularly. Cook the tomato paste, Worcestershire sauce, and fresh thyme for about two to three minutes, or until the tomato paste begins to soften.
5. Cook the red wine for about 3 minutes, scraping up any browned pieces as you go. Beef broth can be used in place of wine if you prefer. Use a wooden spoon to avoid scratching the Dutch oven or pot, just a quick advice.
6. Stir in the flour to coat. Stir in 4 cups of beef broth after adding the flour until the mixture begins to thicken. Add the chopped potatoes, seared meat, and bay leaves. Add extra broth if necessary if it is too thick. After bringing to a boil, lower the heat and simmer for 5-7 minutes. If necessary, add additional salt and pepper at this time.
7. Use an oven-safe lid to cover. Finish cooking the beef in the oven at 300 degrees Fahrenheit for approximately 1 hour and 40 minutes, or until it is tender. 10 minutes before the cooking time is up, add peas, if preferred.
8. Before serving, take off the bay leaves. Serve with some chopped parsley.

NOTES

○ A big lidded Dutch oven. A 6 qt Dutch oven is what I use.
○ To scrape the brown parts from the pot, use wooden spoons. The coating of the Dutch oven won't be scratched.
○ Russet potatoes should be avoided as they are readily broken down. Use red or Yukon gold potatoes.
○ Use airtight containers to store in the refrigerator for up to 3 days.

- For up to 3 months, freeze in freezer-friendly containers. Thaw in the refrigerator overnight before reheating. Reheat in the microwave or on the stovetop after it has thawed.

FRENCH ONION SOUP

INGREDIENTS

- 4 tbsp of unsalted butter
- Vegetable oil, 1 tbsp.
- 3 pounds of Vidalia onions, cut in half lengthwise, then thinly sliced.
- 3/4 tsp of salt
- 1/2 tsp. of freshly ground black pepper.
- 3/4 teaspoon sugar, granulated.
- 1 glass of dry white wine.
- All-purpose flour, 2 tbsp.
- 6 cups of beef broth
- 1 tsp. Worcestershire sauce
- 1/2 tsp. dry thyme
- 2 leaves of bay.
- Sliced into 1-inch pieces, 1 small baguette.
- 1 teaspoon dry sherry
- 8 ounces of grated Gruyère cheese.
- 1/2 cup of grated Parmigiano Reggiano.

INSTRUCTIONS

1. Melt the butter over medium heat in a sizable Dutch oven or soup pot. Add the sugar, salt, pepper, and onions to the oil. Cook onions for 45 to 55 minutes, turning regularly with a wooden spoon until they are a deep golden brown and have caramelized. You will initially simply need to stir the onions occasionally. You will need to stir them frequently when they begin to brown in the middle of cooking, scraping the fond from the bottom of the pan. Reduce the heat a little or add a little water to the pan to deglaze it if the onions are browning too quickly and go on cooking.
2. Turn up the heat and then add the wine. Cook for 8 to 10 minutes, stirring frequently and scraping any fond from the bottom of the pan, or until almost all the liquid has evaporated and the onions are jammy.
3. Cook the flour for one minute while continuously stirring.

4. In the pot, combine the broth, Worcestershire sauce, thyme, and bay leaves. Bring to a boil, lower the heat to a simmer, and cook for about 30 minutes with the lid on.

5. Set an oven rack in the center and heat the oven to 400°F while the soup simmers. In a single layer on a baking sheet, place the baguette pieces. Bake for 10 minutes, or until the bread is crisp, dry, and golden around the edges. Place aside.

6. After the soup has completed cooking, take out the bay leaves, add the sherry, taste, and, if required, adjust the seasoning. Try adding a few shakes of Worcestershire sauce to the soup if it requires a richer taste. Add 1/4 teaspoon sugar if you feel it's not quite sweet enough.

7. Heat the broiler and adjust the oven rack so that it is 6 inches from the element. Divide the hot soup among the individual broiler-safe crocks that have been placed on a baking sheet. Make sure the soup is quite hot because it won't warm up much in the oven. Each crock should have 1 or 2 baguette pieces on top. The cheese should melt and bubble around the edges in the oven after 3 to 5 minutes of broiling the crocks. Before serving, let the crocks cool for a short while.

8. Make-Ahead Directions: The soup can be prepared up to 3 days in advance and refrigerated, or up to 3 months in advance and frozen. Without the cheese, toast can be prepared and stored in a sealed container at room temperature for up to 3 days.

LAMB STEW RECIPE

Prep Time: 20 mins

Cook Time: 2 Hours 20 mins

Total Time: 2 hr. 40 mins

Servings: 8 People

INGREDIENTS

- Bacon: 4 strips, 4 oz., cut into 1/4-inch strips.
- 2 pounds. of boneless, fat-trimmed lamb shoulder or leg, divided into 1 1/2 pieces.
- 1/2 teaspoon of sea salt for the lamb and 1 teaspoon for the stew.
- 1 teaspoon black pepper for the lamb and 1/2 teaspoon for the stew.
- All-purpose flour or gluten-free flour, 1/4 cup.
- 1 big, chopped yellow onion.
- 4 minced garlic cloves
- 1 1/2 cups fine red wine.
- 1 lb. of sliced button mushrooms.
- 4 cups of stock or broth with low sodium meat.
- 1 tablespoon tomato paste
- 2 leaves of bay.
- 1/2 teaspoon dried thyme.
- 1 1/2 lbs. of small yellow potatoes, cut into halves or halves 1 pieces.
- 10 ounces of four medium carrots, peeled and sliced into 1/2 chunky bits
- For garnish, use 1/4 cup of freshly chopped parsley.

INSTRUCTIONS

1. Chop bacon and cook it in a 5 Qt Dutch oven over medium heat until it is browned and the fat has rendered. Transfer the bacon to a sizable plate using a slotted spoon.
2. Season the lamb chunks with 1/2 tbsp salt and 1 tsp pepper as the bacon cooks. Add 1/4 cup of flour and stir to combine. Lamb should be cooked in two batches over medium

heat for three to four minutes per side until browned, then transferred to a platter with the bacon.

3. Add the diced onion and cook for 2 minutes. Cook the garlic for one more minute while stirring continuously. Add 1.5 cups of wine and deglaze the pan by scraping the bottom. Sliced mushrooms should be added after the liquid has simmered for a few minutes. Heat the oven to 325 °F.

4. Add 4 cups broth, 1 Tbsp tomato paste, 1 tsp salt, 1/2 tsp pepper, 1/2 tsp dried thyme, and 2 bay leaves to the saucepan with the bacon and lamb once more. Make sure the potatoes are mostly soaked in liquid before adding the carrots and potatoes. Bring to a boil, then gently move to a preheated 325°F oven for 1 hour and 45 minutes while COVERED. Lamb and potatoes will be quite tender when finished.

NOTES:

- o "Soft Red" wine was what we used. Pinot Noir would also be suitable.
- o When the stew comes out of the oven, spoon any extra oil from the top for a reduced fat stew.

PASTA FAGIOLI SOUP

Prep: 30 Mins

Cook Time: 1 Hr.

Total: 1 Hr. 30 Mins

Servings: 6

INGREDIENTS

- Olive oil, 1 tbsp.
- Diced 1 1/2 ounces of thick-cut bacon.
- 1 pound of crumbled Italian sausage.
- 3 carrots, peeled and chopped, medium size
- 5 medium celery stalks, diced, 1 1/2 cups.
- 1 1/2 cups 2 small to medium-sized onions, chopped and peeled
- 4 peeled and chopped garlic cloves.
- tomatoes paste, 2 tbsp.
- 1 tbsp of Italian seasoning.
- 1/2 tsp. garlic powder
- More broth or a 1/2 cup of red wine.
- 1 can of 24-ounce tomato sauce.
- For additional flavor, use fire-roasted chopped tomatoes in one 15-oz can.
- 5 cups of chicken broth, plus more as necessary.
- To taste, add salt and black pepper.
- 1 cup of dry ditalini pasta.
- 1 15-oz can have washed and drained dark red kidney beans
- 1 rinsed and drained 15-oz can of white cannellini beans.
- To serve, grated parmesan.
- to be served, chopped parsley.

INSTRUCTIONS

1. In a big Dutch oven, warm the olive oil over medium-high heat. For about 3 to 4 minutes, add the bacon and heat until it is browned. Add the sausage and cook for a further 4-5 minutes, or until it is browned as well.

2. The veggies should be sautéed: Add the carrots, celery, onions, and garlic and simmer for 4-5 minutes, or until they begin to soften.

3. Once dispersed equally, stir in the tomato paste, Italian seasoning, and garlic powder. Pour the red wine into the pan and cook it for one minute while scraping the browned bits from the bottom of the pan.

4. Prepare the soup: Chicken stock, tomato sauce, diced tomatoes, salt, and pepper should all be added to the pot. Stir thoroughly then bring to a boil. Cover the pot and lower the heat to a gentle simmer. 15 to 20 minutes of cooking.

5. Uncooked Ditalini should be added to the broth and cooked for 10 minutes uncovered. Once the pasta is cooked and the beans are warmed through, toss in the drained beans and simmer for an additional 4-5 minutes, adding more liquid if necessary. If preferred, garnish right away with parmesan and fresh parsley. Keep leftovers in the fridge for up to 3 days.

NOTES

o Choose a level of spice that you enjoy, whether it be mild or hot. When using whole sausages, just remove the casings and use the sausage meat alone. It must be well broken up during browning, although it functions similarly to ground sausage.

o Pancetta would be ideal in this case, but thick-cut ordinary bacon would also work. If you're not a fan, skip it.

o Great Northern, pale red kidneys, and white kidneys are more options.

o You can use any short, tiny pasta shape. In an earlier iteration of this soup, I used to cook the pasta separately, but I discovered that it wasn't necessary to dirty another pot and now cook the pasta right in the soup. Unless you intend to freeze the soup or abhor soft spaghetti, there is really no need to prepare the noodles separately.

o Wine: The wine does deepen the flavor, but if you don't want to consume alcohol, you can omit it. Use a dry red wine that you would like to drink while making your selection of wine. Although Sangiovese or Chianti would be ideal, you may get away with using a Cabernet Sauvignon, Merlot, or Pinot Noir instead.

- To make the soup more palatable, chop the veggies as uniformly as you can, roughly between the size of the pasta and the beans.
- Browning: Maintain a medium-high or slightly lower heat. Keep cooking the sausage until it gets a lovely caramelized color, even if it appears to be cooked but is still pale. You will absolutely need to take the sausage, wash the pot, remove the worst burned portions of the sausage, and then then proceed with the procedure to salvage it if you heed my warning against using medium-high heat and burn it.
- Although the soup freezes nicely, I do strongly advise leaving out the noodles in this instance. For specific freezer instructions and advice, see the post's notes.

CHAPTER 5: BREAD

DUTCH OVEN CARAWAY RYE BREAD

Prep: 15 mins

Cook: 35 mins

Additional: 18 hrs. 15 mins

Total: 19 hrs. 5 mins

Servings: 12

Make: 1 loaf

INGREDIENTS

- 2 cups of light rye flour
- 2 cups of bread flour
- ¼ cup of buttermilk
- 2 tbsp. caraway seeds
- 1 ½ tbsp. vital wheat gluten
- 2 tbsp crushed flaked kosher salt
- 1 ¾ cups of warm water
- 2 tsp white sugar
- ⅜ tsp active dry yeast

INSTRUCTION

1. In a very large bowl, mix the rye flour, bread flour, buttermilk, caraway seeds, vital wheat gluten, and kosher salt.
2. Until the yeast softens and starts to produce a creamy foam, around 5 minutes, combine the water, sugar, and yeast in a bowl. Stir the yeast mixture into the flour mixture until the caraway seeds are thoroughly combined. For 18 hours, wrap plastic wrap tightly around the bowl.
3. Transfer the dough to a work surface that has been generously dusted with flour. Because it will be somewhat extended, fold the right and left sides into the center. After

flipping the dough over and using a spatula to delicately tuck in the corners, 15 minutes of plastic wrap are required. Remove the plastic wrap, flour the dough, then score the top of the dough to allow for full bloom.

4. Set a Dutch oven inside the oven and heat it to 500 degrees Fahrenheit (260 degrees C).
5. Place the dough in the Dutch oven with care, cover right away, lower the oven's temperature to 460 degrees F (238 degrees C), and bake for 30 to 35 minutes, or until the bread is thoroughly cooked. Bread should be carefully moved from the Dutch oven to the oven rack and baked for an additional 5 minutes.

NOTE

- Feel free to change this as you see fit. I also make white bread with the same recipe. I prefer to substitute 1/4 cup hand-crushed whole oats and a couple tablespoons of bran flake into my white bread recipe. provides pleasing color and texture.
- I wanted this to be relatively simple because traditional rye breads call for sourdough, which is difficult to manage. In order to assist the flavor develop while the dough develops and ferments, I replace 1/4 cup of water with buttermilk.

CRUSTY DUTCH OVEN BREAD

Prep: 30 mins

Cook: 55 mins

Additional: 1 hr. 45 mins

Total: 3 hrs. 10 mins

Servings: 12

Makes: 1 loaf

INGREDIENTS

- 4 cups of bread flour
- 1 ½ cups of water
- 2 tsp. salt
- 1 tsp. active dry yeast

INSTRUCTION

1. Salt and water are then added to the bowl of an electric stand mixer after the bread flour has been added. Spread the yeast over the top and sprinkle it 5 minutes to dissolve.
2. Until the dough comes together, mix with the paddle attachment at medium speed. Dough hook in its position, replace the paddle. For about 10 minutes, keep on mixing until the dough is elastic and smooth.
3. After giving the dough 30 to 45 minutes to rise to roughly twice its original size, cover the bowl with plastic wrap. A finger is pushed into the dough. The dough should resist a little but not rebound. If it bounces back, give it more time to rise.
4. To release extra gas and redistribute the yeast, turn the dough out onto a surface that has been dusted with flour. For 10 to 15 minutes, cover with a clean dish towel and allow to rest. •

5. Push the dough in a circular motion back and forth on the counter until it forms a smooth, spherical ball. Allow the dough to rise for about an hour, covered with a clean dish towel.

6. Set the oven's temperature to 230 Celsius. Dutch oven: grease it.

7. Sharpen your knife and cut a very shallow "X" into the bread's top to aid in its expansion during baking. Insert the bread into the Dutch oven that has been prepared and secure the lid.

8. For 10 minutes, bake in the preheated oven. Bake for another 20 minutes with the cover on at 190 degrees C. After 25 to 30 minutes, remove the lid and keep baking until the food is deeply golden.

DUTCH OVEN WHOLE WHEAT BREAD

Prep Time: 15 mins

Cook Time: 40 mins

Additional Time: 8 hrs. 45 mins

Total Time: 9 hrs. 40 mins

Servings: 10

INGREDIENTS

- 1 ½ cups of warm water
- 1 tsp. active dry yeast
- 1 tsp. agave nectar
- 3 cups of whole wheat flour
- ½ tsp. salt

INSTRUCTION

1. In a measuring cup that is microwave-safe, pour water and heat for about a minute. To ensure that the water is not hotter than 38 degrees C, use a food thermometer to check the temperature. Add the yeast and agave; allow to stand for 15 minutes or until frothy.
2. In a large bowl, combine the flour and salt. Add the yeast mixture and give it a few kneads to combine. Dough should rise overnight to 18 hours in a warm environment with the bowl covered.
3. On a floured surface, spread the dough out. Use floured hands to knead the dough 5 to 10 times. While the oven is heating up, form the dough into a ball and let it rise.
4. A Dutch oven should be heated for 30 minutes at 230 degrees Celsius in the oven.
5. To carefully drop dough into the heated Dutch oven, use floured hands. Put the Dutch oven's cover on using potholders.
6. Bake for 30 minutes in the hot oven. Bake the bread for a further 10 to 15 minutes after removing the Dutch oven's cover. Remove and allow cooling.

MULTI-SEED NO-KNEAD DUTCH OVEN BREAD RECIPE

Prep Time 10 Minutes

Cook Time 35 Minutes

Yield 1 Loaf

Makes: 10 Pieces

INGREDIENTS

- 1 ½ cups and 2 tbsp warm water.
- 2 ¼ tsp of rapid rising yeast
- 3 tbsp sugar
- 3 cups of bread flour
- 1 tsp. salt
- 2 tbsp. almond slices
- 1 ½ tbsp. pumpkin seeds
- 1 tbsp. sunflower seeds
- 1 tbsp. flax seeds
- 1 tbsp. chia seeds

INSTRUCTIONS

1. Combine the flour and seeds in a large bowl, then create a well in the middle.
2. Combine warm water, sugar, yeast, and salt in a medium bowl. Combine by whisking.
3. Fill the well in the large bowl with the water-yeast mixture.
4. Once a dough starts to form, stir with a wooden spoon to help it along.
5. Transfer the dough to a floured surface and knead it for 3 minutes, or until there are no longer any flour streaks. If it is too sticky, add more flour; if it is too dry, add more water. The dough will be soft and seem something between rough and smooth.

6. Form the dough into a rough round and place it in a bowl that has been lightly greased. Wrap the food carefully in plastic wrap and a cloth or tea towel. Allow the dough to double in size by rising at room temperature for 1 1/2 to 2 hours in a warm location.
7. Set the oven to 450 degrees.
8. The dough should be taken out of the bowl and put on a floured surface. Form a ball by lightly pressing down, folding the dough's four corners into the center, and squeezing together. It should be taken out of the bowl and placed, smooth side up and seam side down, onto a sheet of parchment paper. With your hands, slightly enlarge the dough ball. After cleaning with water, sprinkle additional seeds on top. Make a small cut through the middle of the loaf using a tiny, sharp paring knife. Place the Dutch oven into the preheated oven for 15 to 20 minutes.
9. Remove the lid from the Dutch oven and take it out of the oven.
10. To carefully insert the dough into the Dutch oven, lift the parchment paper's edges. Recover the lid.
11. After baking for 30 minutes with the lid off, continue baking for 5 more minutes or until nicely golden.

NOTES

- Change, substitute, or add ANY of the nuts and seeds. Pick your preferred flavor and personalize your loaf!
- For this recipe, just use RAPID rising yeast. Regular active dry yeast will increase rising time + alter results.
- Use this bread to make your preferred sandwiches, avocado toast, butter toast, and more!
- By grinding any leftover or stale bread in a blender or food processor and preserving in an airtight container, you may turn it into breadcrumbs.
- Wrap your bread tightly in plastic and keep it there for 2 days at room temperature or 1 month in the freezer. To make things easier if freezing, slice the bread first!
- Bread may soon dry out in the refrigerator; avoid doing this.

EASY DUTCH OVEN BREAD

Prep Time: 2 hours 5 minutes

Cook Time: 45 minutes

Total Times: 2 hours 50 minutes

Servings: 10 slices

INGREDIENTS

- 3 cups of all-purpose flour
- yeast
- salt
- water

INSTRUCTIONS

1. For 45 to 60 seconds, microwave your water to a warm temperature.
2. Whisk the salt and quick-rising yeast together in a mixing bowl until thoroughly combined.
3. Once a shaggy, sticky dough has formed, stir in the flour. If you need to add a little more water to get this combined, don't get upset. (Around 1/2 cup) Humidity levels vary from place to another. You want a texture that is sticky!
4. Place the dish in a warm spot in your kitchen and cover with a tea towel. I prefer to put it next to my oven that is heating up.
5. Approximately 2 hours should pass for this to double in size.
6. To get your Dutch oven piping hot, preheat the oven to 450 degrees Fahrenheit 45 minutes before baking.
7. When it's ready to bake, spread out a piece of parchment paper and sprinkle 1 tablespoon of flour to it.
8. Using a silicone spatula, transfer the rising dough to the parchment paper, and then delicately roll it into a ball.

9. I fold the dough over itself 4 times with my spatula, sort of like folding a letter. Just make sure it is shaped like a round loaf, please.

10. Make a few small cuts in the dough's top with a knife. The lovely form on top will result from the steam being able to exit in this way.

11. Remove the Dutch oven from the oven with caution, taking up the parchment's 4 corners. Place it into the pot with caution.

12. Put everything back in the oven for 35 minutes after replacing the lid with an oven mit.

13. Remove the lid after 35 minutes and continue cooking for a further 10-15 minutes.

14. Remove the bread loaf and parchment with care, then set the dutch oven aside to cool on a chopping board.

DUTCH OVEN MONKEY BREAD

Prep Time: 5 Mins

Cook Time: 15 Mins

Total Time: 20 Mins

Servings: 6

INGREDIENTS

- 4 tbsp. butter
- 1/4 cup of white sugar
- 1/4 cup of brown sugar
- 2 tbsp. cinnamon
- 1/2 cup of chopped walnuts
- 16 ounce of tube refrigerator biscuits
- Powdered sugar glaze

INSTRUCTIONS

1. You can measure and combine the ingredients marked with at home.
2. Dutch oven should be preheated to 350 degrees F (total of 25 coals, 17 on top of lid and 8 below bottom of oven).
3. In a plastic bag, mix cinnamon, white sugar, brown sugar, and nuts.
4. Each biscuit should be broken into small bits. Place biscuit pieces in a bag, seal it securely to prevent a mess, and shake to thoroughly coat.
5. In the Dutch oven, melt the butter.
6. Pour the full contents of the bag into the oven, stir in the butter, and then spread out to cover the bottom of the oven in a uniform layer.
7. For 15 to 25 minutes, or until the dough is done, cover the pan and bake at 350 degrees F. Placement of coals: Make sure to lay the bottom coals in a circle to avoid having a "central coal," since this would cause the middle pieces of bread to burn.
8. To achieve consistent baking, turn the oven's bottom and lid in different directions every 5 minutes.

9. Before serving warm, remove from the heat and allow it cool slightly.

10. If desired, drizzle sugar glaze over the top.

DUTCH-OVEN JALAPENO CHEDDAR BREAD

Total time: 3 hr.

Servings: 8

INGREDIENTS

- 3 ½ cups of bread flour
- 2 ½ cups of shredded sharp cheddar cheese, divided
- 2 jalapenos, seeded and coarsely chopped
- 1 jalapeno, sliced and divided
- 1 tbsp. kosher salt
- 2 cups of warm water
- 2 ¼ tsp. yeast
- 1 tbsp. olive oil

INSTRUCTION

1. Combine the bread flour, 2 cups (200 g) of cheddar cheese, the chopped jalapenos, and salt in a large bowl. Stir thoroughly.
2. Combine the yeast and warm water in a separate, large bowl. Using a silicone spatula, combine the flour mixture with the water and stir until the dough comes together.
3. Fold the dough 8 times around the perimeter of the bowl with the spatula, rotating the bowl each time you fold. In a warm location, cover with a kitchen towel and leave for 60 minutes, or until almost doubled in size.
4. Fold the dough 8 more times toward the center while using the spatula. For 30 minutes, wrap in the towel and allow to relax.
5. After placing the Dutch oven and lid inside, turn the oven on for 30 minutes at 450°F (230°C).
6. Flour your hands and a spotless work surface. Peel the dough slowly from the bowl and place it on the floured surface. Turnover, then remove any extra flour with a soft brush. 8 times fold the dough's sides toward the center, then turn it over and place it on a sheet of parchment paper.

7. Olive oil should be brushed over the dough's top so the cheese will adhere. Top with the remaining 50 g (or 1/2 cup) of cheese. To create a "X" in the bread that will allow steam to escape, use a sharp knife. Place the cheese on top of the jalapeno rings.

8. Remove the Dutch oven from the oven with care, then carefully lift the bread into the pot using the parchment. Bake the bread for a further 20 minutes without the lid after the initial 30 minutes, or until golden brown.

9. Slide the bread carefully onto a wire rack after removing it from the pot. Before slicing the bread, take the parchment paper off and allow it to cool for at least one hour.

10. Bread should be sliced and served as desired.

11. Enjoy!

IRISH SODA BREAD

Prep Time: 5 Mins

Cook Time: 55 Mins

Total Time: 1 Hr.

Servings: 1 Loaf

INGREDIENTS

- 3 1/2 cups of flour
- 1 tsp. baking soda
- 1 1/2 tsp. salt
- 1 1/2 cups of buttermilk

INSTRUCTIONS

1. For at least 15 minutes, preheat the oven to 450 degrees Fahrenheit. No need to trim the parchment paper; simply cover the bottom of a large (5 qt) Dutch oven or cast iron and set aside.
2. Combine all the dry ingredients in a large bowl. Use your fingers to mix in the buttermilk gradually until a dough forms and neither the flour nor the buttermilk are visible. As soon as the dough begins to come together, stop touching it for a rustic loaf. You can fold the dough for an additional 20 seconds if you want a finer crumb and smoother crust. It should be roughly formed into a ball before being placed in the Dutch oven.
3. Score a cross into the top with a sharp knife, wiping the blade between each incision.
4. For about 45 minutes, bake with a cover until it has risen. After about 10 to 15 more minutes of baking, remove the lid and continue baking until the food is golden brown. Take it out of the oven and allow it to cool a little in the Dutch oven. Before serving, allow the food to chill for at least 30 minutes on a cooler rack.
5. Serve it hot, with butter, or as a side dish for soups and stews!

PUMPKIN BLUEBERRY BREAD

Prep Time: 20 Minutes

Cook Time: 1 Hour

Serves 8

INGREDIENTS

- 2 eggs
- 1 cup of canned pumpkin
- 1 cup sugar
- ½ cup of vegetable oil
- 2 cups of all-purpose flour
- 1½ tsp. pumpkin pie spice
- 1 tsp. baking soda
- ½ tsp. salt
- 1 cup of fresh blueberries, divided
- 1 tbsp. of all-purpose flour
- Cooking spray

INSTRUCTION

1. The oven should be heated to 325°F.
2. Mix the eggs, sugar, pumpkin, and vegetable oil in a medium bowl.
3. Stir the flour, pumpkin pie spice, baking soda, and salt in a large bowl. Stir after adding the pumpkin mixture to the flour mixture.
4. The blueberries and the tablespoon of flour should be combined in a small bowl and gently mixed.
5. 2/3 cup of blueberries are then gently incorporated into the batter.
6. Spoon the batter in a Dutch oven that has been sprayed with cooking spray. Add the final 1/3 cup of blueberries on top.
7. A toothpick should come out clean after roughly an hour of baking under cover in the oven.

NOTE

- o Allow the bread to cool in the Dutch oven for about 10 minutes before removing it. The bread can then be gently removed from the pan with a wide spatula made of wood, plastic, or both, and finished cooling on a wire rack.

CHAPTER 6: BEEF

BEEF CURRY

Prep time: 20 mins

Cook time: 2 hrs.15 mins

Servings: 4

INGREDIENTS

- 1 lb. ground beef.
- 1 onion diced.
- 2 celery stalks, trimmed and diced.
- 1 large carrot, cut and clipped.
- 1/2 cup of Frozen Garden peas.
- 1/2 tsp of garlic powder.
- 1/4 tsp of ground ginger.
- 1 1/2 tsp of curry powder on medium heat.
- Uncooked basmati rice, 1 1/2 cups.
- 1/2 cups of water.
- 1/4 tsp of salt.

INSTRUCTION

1. Get ready to cook over your campfire.
2. A 12-in (30.5-cm) Dutch oven with 6 coals surrounding it and 18 on the lid is required. A cooking temperature of 350°F (177°C) is preferred.
3. Break up the ground beef with a wooden spoon before adding it to the Dutch oven. Stir until evenly browned.
4. Add the onion, celery, and carrot and simmer for 3 minutes while stirring.
5. After that, add the peas, curry powder, ground ginger, and garlic powder and mix everything together thoroughly for 2–3 minutes.
6. Add the water after stirring the basmati rice. Bring the mixture to a boil while stirring to incorporate.
7. After giving the curry a taste, add salt

8. Put the Dutch oven's lid on and move it further away from the center of the coals to lower the heat.
9. Stir the curry occasionally while letting it simmer for 10-15 minutes or until the rice is done. The entire cooking time will be 35 to 40 minutes.
10. Enjoy after serving.

DUTCH OVEN MEATLOAF

Prep Time: 10 minutes

Cook Time: 1 hour 30 minutes

Additional Time: 10 minutes

Total Time: 1 hour 50 minutes

INGREDIENT

- 1 1/2 lbs. of ground beef.
- 1 lb. of Italian sausage, ground.
- 1 tbsp. of garlic mince.
- 1 tbsp. Celtic salt
- 1 tbsp. of minced onion.
- 1 tsp black pepper, ground.
- 1 tsp. dried basil
- 1 tsp. oregano, dried.
- 1/2 of dried rosemary
- 1 tsp. dried parsley
- 1/2 tsp. of dried thyme
- 3 big-sized eggs.
- 1/2 cup of half and half.
- 1 cup of parmesan cheese, grated.
- Glaze for meatloaf.
- 1/4 cup of tomato paste.
- 2 tsp of Worcestershire sauce.
- 1 tsp apple cider vinegar
- 1 teaspoon honey.
- 3 tbsp. of beef broth.

INSTRUCTIONS

1. Set the oven's temperature to 350 °F. Set out the mixing basins and dutch oven along with all the ingredients.

2. Salt, pepper, herbs, and spices should all be combined thoroughly in a small mixing dish. Mix in the parmesan cheese.
3. Add the half-and-half and three large eggs to a different bowl. Mix until thoroughly combined and eggs are beaten in.
4. The meat should be mixed with your hands for the finest results. Mix the ground meats—ground beef and ground sausage—in a sizable mixing basin. If you'd rather not use your hands, you may also mix the meat with a wooden spoon or a potato masher.
5. Add the herbs, spices, and egg mixture after the meat has been combined. All ingredients should be thoroughly combined.
6. Shape the meat mixture into a 9" x 5" loaf. Just enough pressure is needed to hold the meatloaf together without making it too dense. Put the loaf in a loaf pan or Dutch oven made of cast iron.
7. The meatloaf in the Dutch oven should be baked for one hour and fifteen minutes.
8. Combine the ingredients for the glaze while the meatloaf bakes. To make a homemade ketchup glaze, mix tomato paste, Worcestershire sauce, apple cider vinegar, honey, and beef broth.
9. Remove the meatloaf from the oven after an hour and fifteen minutes of baking. Remove the excess fat from the meatloaf's top and drain the grease from the Dutch oven's bottom.
10. The meatloaf should then have glaze applied to it. For a further 15 minutes, place the meatloaf back in the oven without a cover.
11. The meatloaf's internal temperature is the finest and most reliable indicator of doneness. It's time to remove the meatloaf from the oven when it reaches 160°F.
12. Prior to slicing and serving meatloaf, the meat must be let to rest for a few minutes. By doing this, the meatloaf's cooked-in liquids can be distributed and allowed to settle. As a result, the end product is juicy, moist, and simple to cut.

NOTES

- o A meatloaf that has been overmixed will be dense and dry.
- o Your hands are the best tools for the task when it comes to creating meatloaf! Mix everything until well combined, but try not to squish or pack the loaf too tightly as this will make the meat firm and dense.

- The majority of recipes ask for using simply ground beef, but my version also calls for using ground sausage. This is the tastiest meatloaf made in a Dutch oven because the ground sausage provides such a wonderful taste.

DUTCH OVEN CHILI MAC

Prep Time: 5 Mins

Cook Time: 40 Mins

Total Time: 45 Mins

Servings: 6

INGREDIENTS

- 1 tbsp. of olive oil.
- 1 medium diced onion.
- 2 minced garlic cloves.
- 1 lb. of ground beef
- 1/2 tsp of salt.
- 1/ tsp. of black pepper.
- 1 can 14 oz. beef broth.
- 1 package of elbow macaroni (16 oz.)
- 1 can of undrained kidney beans (14.50 oz.).
- 1 can of undrained pinto beans (14.5 oz.).
- 1 can of undrained fire-roasted diced tomatoes (14.5 oz.).
- 1 can of diced green Chile peppers (4 oz.).
- 1 cup of cheddar cheese, shredded.

INSTRUCTIONS

1. Heat the oil in a 12-inch Dutch oven over medium heat. Stir for about 5 minutes after stirring the onion and garlic.
2. Using a spoon, crumble the ground beef and add it along with the salt and pepper. Cook the meat for another 15 minutes, stirring frequently, until it has browned.
3. stir the green Chile peppers, tomatoes, beans, macaroni, and broth. For about 10 minutes, bring the mixture to a boil while stirring often to prevent the pasta from sticking to the bottom of the pot.

4. Place the lid on the Dutch oven and cook for 8 to 10 minutes, or until the macaroni is the desired tenderness, stirring occasionally to prevent the mac and cheese from sticking to the bottom.
5. Serve hot with cheddar cheese on top.

NOTES

- o Simply add a little more liquid (water is OK) to the pan to continue the boiling process until the pasta is as tender as you prefer if the liquid is reducing too quickly and the pasta needs to cook for longer.

BEEF BOURGUIGNON

Prep Time: 30 Mins

Cook Time: 4 Hrs.

Total Time: 4 Hrs. 30 Mins

Servings: 10

INGREDIENT

To make the marinade:

- 3 lbs. of stew beef.
- 1 bottle of red wine bottle, 750 ml.
- 1 tbsp. of garlic powder.
- 1 tbsp. of powdered onion.
- Fresh parsley, 1 tbsp.
- 2 tbsp. of sugar.
- 1 tsp of Worcestershire sauce
- Himalayan sea salt, 1/2 teaspoon.
- 1/2 tsp. of red pepper flakes.
- Water to cover meat.

Sachet of spices:

- 6 garlic cloves.
- 2 leaves of bay.
- 2 tbsp. of fresh thyme.
- 1 tsp Tellicherry Black Pepper, freshly ground.
- beef bourguignon.
- Vegetable oil, tbsp.
- Himalayan sea salt, 1/4 tsp.
- 1/4 of Tellicherry black pepper, freshly ground.
- 3 lbs. of chunky marinated beef stew.
- 2 cups of water.

Sachet:

- 1 packet or 1 cup of homemade Demi-Glace.
- 475 gm or 1 pint of mushrooms
- Butter, 4 tbsp.
- 1/4 cup of flour

INSTRUCTIONS

1. Put all the marinade ingredients in a big bowl and use that to marinade the meat. Mix thoroughly, cover, and chill for up to 2 days in the refrigerator.

2. Heat the vegetable oil in a Dutch oven over medium heat. Carefully put the meat to the oil using a slotted spoon, reserving the marinade for later. While the steak is cooking, season it with salt and pepper after searing each side. The cooked, browned meat should be placed in another bowl and left aside. Any juice should stay in the Dutch oven's bottom.

3. The wine marinade, water, spice sachet, demi-glace, and mushrooms should all be added to the Dutch oven. 20 minutes or so of boiling should result in reduction. Reintroduce the browned meat to the pot, then top with a lid. The beef should be fork tender and falling apart after 2.5 hours in an oven preheated to 375 degrees Fahrenheit.

4. Reposition the pot on the stovetop. The broth should remain in the pot's bottom after you remove the meat from it once more and discard the sachet. Reducing the sauce once more to around 4 cups over medium heat.

5. Melt the butter in a different saucepan, then whisk in the flour to stir a roux. Stirring continuously will cause the sauce to thicken. Slowly whisk the roux into the Dutch oven sauce. Reintroduce the meat into the sauce to completely reheat it. Enjoy with potatoes au gratin when served!

HERB-CRUSTED ROAST BEEF & POTATOES

Prep Time: 10 Minutes

Cook Time: 1 Hr. 15 mins

Serves: 6

INGREDIENT

- 12 new potatoes (1-1/2 pounds)
- 1 tsp of sea salt.
- 1 tsp of sea salt.
- 4 minced garlic cloves
- 1 tsp. dried thyme
- 1 tsp of rosemary, dry.
- Dijon mustard, 2 tbsp.
- 3 lbs. of round roast eye

INSTRUCTION

1. Set the oven to 325 F.
2. Boil water in a Dutch oven over medium heat. The potatoes should only just be barely cooked through after being boiled. Place in a bowl.
3. Spread a paste made of the salt, pepper, garlic, thyme, rosemary, and mustard over the roast. Place the meat, fat side up, in the Dutch oven and roast for about 20 minutes per pound, or until the internal temperature 125°F for rare, 150°F for medium, or 160°F for well-done.
4. The potatoes should be added to the pot and turned on all sides about 30 minutes before the beef is cooked to your preference.

BEEF TENDERLOIN

Prep Time: 15 Minutes

Cook Time: 1 Hr. 30 minutes

Serves: 6

INGREDIENT

- 3/4 lbs. of shallots, peeled and halved lengthwise
- 1 1/2 tsp. of tomato paste
- 3 slices of bacon, diced.
- 1 (2 pounds) beef tenderloin.
- 1 tsp. of thyme, dried
- 2 tbsp. butter, softened.
- 1 tbsp. of all-purpose flour
- 2 tbsp. extra-virgin divided olive oil.
- Salt
- black pepper, freshly ground
- 3 cups of beef stock or broth.

INSTRUCTION

1. the oven to 350 degrees Fahrenheit.
2. 1 tbsp of olive oil and the shallots should be combined in a Dutch oven. Add salt and pepper to taste. For about 30 minutes, or until the shallots are browned, bake in the preheated oven. Place on a plate.
3. Over high heat, bring the broth to a boil in the Dutch oven. After adding the tomato paste, stir the mixture and transfer it to a bowl.
4. Cook the bacon in the pot with the remaining 1 tablespoon olive oil over medium heat for 7 to 10 minutes, or until it is browned and crispy. Place on the serving dish with the shallots.

5. Salt, pepper, and thyme are used to season the tenderloin. Add to the pot and simmer for 7 minutes, stirring occasionally, until evenly browned. Bake with a cover on for 25 minutes, or until medium-rare or an internal thermometer reads 130–135°F.

6. The tenderloin should be moved to a platter. Return the pot to the stovetop after skimming off any extra fat. Return the broth mixture to the pot and bring to a boil while using a wooden spoon to scrape any browned bits from the pot's bottom and edges. Set the thermostat to low. Cook for 2 to three minutes, or until the sauce thickens, after whisking in the butter and flour. Bring the bacon and shallots back to the saucepan. Add salt and pepper to taste.

7. Slices of the tenderloin should be 12 inches thick. Place in a serving dish, then drizzle sauce over top.

NOTE

o   A few watercress sprigs provide a wonderful garnish for this hearty entrée. To complete the meal, serve potatoes and grilled asparagus as side dishes.

BEER-BRAISED BEEF SHORT RIBS

Prep Time: 30 Mins

Cook Time: 3 Hrs.

Total Time: 3 Hrs. 35 Mins

Servings: 6

INGREDIENTS

- 3 to 4 pounds of bone-in short ribs of beef
- 2 large of yellow onions.
- 5-6 big carrots, cut on the bias into 1-inch chunks.
- 5 cloves garlic, minced
- 1 cup chopped tomatoes
- 1 ½ cups of craft beer
- 2 tsp. of Dijon mustard
- 4-5 sprigs of fresh Thyme, tied in a bundle
- 2-3 tbsp of avocado, canola or vegetable neutral oil for searing.
- salt and pepper as needed.

INSTRUCTION

1. Set the oven's temperature to 325.
2. With a paper towel, pat the short ribs dry before lightly seasoning them with salt and pepper.
3. onion rings that are 1/2 inch thick. Carrots should be peeled and sliced on the bias into bits measuring 1 inch. minced cloves of garlic. Separate the vegetables.
4. In a sizzling hot big skillet, preferably made of cast iron, heat a couple of teaspoons of avocado oil. Short ribs should be seared until a brown crust form all over. Transfer the ingredients to a big Dutch oven in stages as you go. This process will take 7-8 minutes.

5. Lower the heat in the same skillet and add the onions once the ribs have been browned in the Dutch oven. until they are browned but not scorched, cook them down. 6 to 8 minutes.

6. Once the onions are aromatic, add the minced garlic and simmer for another minute.

7. To deglaze the pan, add beer and crushed tomatoes to the skillet. Using a wooden spoon, stir while scraping off all of the brown residue from the pan's bottom.

8. To the onion mixture, add the Dijon mustard and season once more with salt and pepper. Increase the heat to medium-high. To allow flavors to mingle, stir and boil for 3–4 minutes. For seasoning, taste.

9. In the Dutch oven, arrange the cooked short ribs on top of the raw carrot chunks. Over the short ribs and carrots in the Dutch oven, carefully pour the skillet's contents.

10. Tie rope around 5–6 fresh thyme sprigs. If you don't have any twine, I tie it together numerous times using a few extra-sturdy thyme stems. Then, cover the Dutch oven with the thyme bundle.

11. Until the meat barely clings to the bone, bake covered with the lid in the oven for 2 1/2 to 3 hours. With tongs, turn the ribs in the sauce halfway through cooking.

12. Take the bundled thyme out of the pot and throw it away.

13. On a bed of creamy parmesan polenta or garlic mashed potatoes, serve the short ribs.

NOTES

o The short ribs must bake covered, so check that your Dutch oven has a heat-safe knob! Up to a particular temperature, most of them work.

o This is a recipe that tastes even better the next day, so it's a perfect one to prepare ahead of time. If any fat forms on the top after cooking the ribs overnight, skim it off. Then, before serving, gently reheat the ribs on the stove in a heavy-bottomed pot.

ROAST BEEF WITH ROOT VEGETABLES

Prep Time: 20 Minutes

Cook Time: 1 Hr. 30 Minutes

Servings: 7

INGREDIENT

- 6 minced garlic cloves.
- 2 tbsp. of whole-grain or Dijon mustard
- 2 tbsp of sea salt, divided, plus a pinch.
- 2 tablespoons freshly ground black pepper.
- 1 tbsp thyme, dried.
- 1/4 cup of extra-virgin olive oil.
- 1 boneless prime rib roast beef, 4 lbs.
- 1 1/2 lbs. of halved potatoes.
- 1/2 lb. of beets, sliced and peeled.
- 1/2 lb. of turnips, peeled and sliced
- 1/2 lb. of parsnips, sliced and peeled.

INSTRUCTION

1. The oven should be heated to 325°F.
2. To combine a rub, mix the garlic, mustard, 2 teaspoons each of salt and pepper, thyme, and 2 cup olive oil in a small bowl. The prime rib should be well patted after applying the rub evenly. Place the fat-side up of the roast in the Dutch oven.
3. Combine the potatoes, beets, turnips, and parsnips in a bowl with the final 3 tablespoons of olive oil, the salt, and the pepper. The vegetables should be placed around the prime rib.
4. For medium-rare, roast for about 20 minutes per pound in a preheated oven, or until the internal temperature reaches 130°F. It should be removed at 150°F if you desire a medium roast. To preserve the juices, let the roast rest for 20 minutes before carving.

NOTES

- o To guarantee consistent cooking, roasts should be nearly at room temperature before baking.
- o At least 30 minutes before cooking, remove the roast from the fridge.

DUTCH OVEN MEATBALLS

Prep Time: 20 minutes

Cook Time: 30 minutes

Total Time: 50 minutes

Servings: 6 people

INGREDIENTS

- 1 cup of Italian breadcrumbs
- 1 tbsp. of milk
- 1 lb. of 80% ground beef, lean.
- 1 lb. of ground pork
- 1/4 cup of minced yellow onion.
- 2 cloves garlic, minced
- 2 tbsp. of chopped flat-leaf parsley.
- 2 large eggs.
- 1/2 cup of parmesan cheese, shredded.
- 2 bay leaves, whole
- 1/2 tsp of red pepper, crushed
- 1/2 teaspoon of Italian seasoning
- 6-ounces of tomato paste, canned.
- 2 of canned crushed tomatoes, 28-ounces
- Pepper and salt for seasoning
- 1 ounce of fresh basil for serving
- 6 small bread loaves.

INSTRUCTIONS

1. Toss the milk with the breadcrumbs in a big bowl and let them soak it up. Add the eggs, parmesan cheese, meat, pork, onion, garlic, parsley, and salt and pepper to the top. Just combine by hand after blending.

2. Make 10 to 12 meatballs with your hands or an ice cream scoop. They should be placed into the bottom of a large pot or 5–7 quart Dutch oven with extreme care. About 5 minutes of browning on medium heat is followed by a gentle spoon turn to brown the opposite side.
3. Make a sauce that is tasty. Add bay leaves, crushed red pepper, Italian seasoning, and a liberal amount of salt and pepper to the same pot as the meatballs. Add tomato paste and chopped tomatoes on top.
4. Cook the meatballs, covered, on low heat for 30 minutes, or until the internal temperature reaches 160°F. Serve meatballs with freshly torn basil and parmesan cheese within toasted white subs.

NOTES

o   Remove the lid after cooking to let the steam out. Allow 10 minutes before attempting to store piping hot sauce because it does not cool well in the freezer. The meatballs will freeze more quickly if you distribute them into sealed bags or containers before freezing. Transfer to the refrigerator 1 day beforehand to defrost. Keep chilled for up to 4 days or freeze for up to 3 months.

DUTCH OVEN BEEF OSSO BUCO

Cook Time: 50 Min

Servings: 4

INGREDIENTS

- 2 lbs. of beef osso Buco.
- 1 tablespoon of butter.
- 2 tablespoons of olive Oil
- 2 minced garlic cloves
- 1/2 diced onion.
- 2 diced medium carrots.
- 1 cup of beef stock
- 1/2 cup of white wine
- 14 oz. of canned diced tomatoes
- 1 teaspoon of Salt
- 1/4 teaspoon of Black Pepper
- 1/4 teaspoon Thyme, Dried.
- 1/8 teaspoon of rosemary, dried.
- 1/8 teaspoon of Oregano
- Chopped Parsley, for Garnish

INSTRUCTION

1. Set the oven to 325 F. Salt and pepper the beef after patting it dry. You can wrap kitchen twine around each cut if you want to serve your osso buco whole.
2. In a 6-quart Dutch oven or other similar-sized pot, melt the butter and oil over medium-high heat. The steak should be seared for 4 minutes per side until browned on both sides. Take out and place aside.
3. The dutch oven should now contain carrots, onions, and garlic. Sauté the ingredients for 5 minutes over medium heat.
4. Add the wine while using a wooden spoon to scrape the pan's bottom. Bring to a simmer the tomatoes, beef stock, meat, and herbs. Cook for 3 hours with a cover on in the oven.

5. Serve with fresh parsley on top of polenta or mashed potatoes.

DUTCH OVEN BEEF ROAST

Cook Time: 2 hrs.

Servings: 4

INGREDIENTS

- 4-5 lbs. of bottom round roast beef.
- 3 sliced and peeled of carrots.
- 4 sweet or russet potatoes, cut.
- 1 diced celeriac.
- 2 quartered onions.
- 3 minced garlic cloves
- 1 tablespoon of tomato paste
- 1/2 cup of red wine.
- 2 cups of beef stock
- 2 leaves of bay.
- fresh sprigs of thyme.
- frying fat
- freshly ground black pepper and sea salt.

INSTRUCTION

1. Set your oven to 350 degrees.
2. Sea salt and freshly ground black pepper should be used to season the beef.
3. In a Dutch oven set over medium-high heat, melt some cooking butter.
4. It takes 1 to 2 minutes per side to brown the roast completely.
5. Cook for 2 to 3 minutes after adding the tomato paste, onion, and garlic.
6. If used, pour the wine in. After cleaning the pan's bottom, boil the dish until it has been cut in half.
7. Add the beef stock, thyme, and bay leaves along with all the vegetables. Simmer, then cover and put in the oven.
8. 2 hours or the meat reaching 145 F should be spent roasting in the oven.

CHAPTER 7: PASTA

VEGGIE PASTA

Prep Time: 10 Mins

Cook Time: 20 Mins

Total Time: 30 Mins

INGREDIENTS

- 2 minced cloves garlic.
- 1 yellow onion, chopped.
- 2 carrots.
- 2 tablespoon of olive oil
- 8 ounces of mushrooms
- 1 medium zucchini.
- 1 red bell pepper
- 1/2 pound of rotini.
- 1/2 teaspoon of basil, dried.
- 1/2 teaspoon of oregano, dried.
- 2 cups of vegetable broth
- 24 ounces of pasta sauce
- 4 ounces of shredded mozzarella.

INSTRUCTIONS

1. The carrots should be sliced, the onion diced, and the garlic minced. Olive oil should be added to a big pot along with the carrots, onion, and garlic. The onions should be sautéed until transparent and tender over medium heat.
2. Slice the mushrooms while the vegetables are sautéing. Sliced vegetables should be added to the pot with the other vegetables and sautéed further.
3. Dice the bell pepper and zucchini while the other vegetables are sautéing.

4. After the zucchini and bell pepper have been diced, add them to the pot along with the rotini, basil, and oregano. To combine, stir. Even if the pasta isn't completely covered by the soup, that's fine.

5. Turn the heat to medium-high, cover the saucepan, and wait for the broth to begin boiling.

6. After the stock has fully boiled, quickly stir the pasta, put the lid back on, and reduce the heat to medium-low. For about 10 minutes, or until the pasta is soft, let the pasta simmer on medium-low, stirring regularly, and always covering the pot with a lid.

7. Add the pasta sauce to the pot and stir to combine once the pasta has cooked through. Re-cover the pot with the lid after adding the cheese shreds on top. Just long enough for the cheese to melt while the pasta is heating. Serve warm!

ONE-POT SPAGHETTI

Cook Time: 20 minutes

Total Time: 30 minutes

Servings: 6

INGREDIENTS

- 1 lb. of ground beef, lean.
- 3 minced cloves garlic.
- freshly ground black pepper and salt as needed.
- 3 cups of marinara sauce.
- 1 tbsp. of tomato paste.
- ½ tsp. of balsamic vinegar
- 1 tsp. of basil, dried.
- ¾ tsp. oregano, dried.
- ¼ tsp. thyme, dried.
- 1-2 tsp. sugar.
- 3 cups of beef broth
- 8 oz. of spaghetti noodles.
- Freshly grated Parmesan cheese.
- Parsley, minced.
- Crushed red pepper flakes.

INSTRUCTION

1. In a big pot or Dutch oven, heat the oil to medium-high. While cooking, break up and stir the ground beef as it cooks until it is no longer pink. Add the minced garlic and stir for one or two more minutes, or until fragrant.
2. After removing the pot's fat, season the beef to taste with salt and pepper. Add the beef broth, tomato paste, balsamic vinegar, dried thyme, dried oregano, dried basil, and

dried marinara sauce. Combine everything thoroughly, come to a boil, and then stir the heat down to a low simmer (about medium-low).

3. Lay the broken spaghetti noodles over the sauce, pressing them down so that they are completely submerged in the sauce. Don't stir at this time.
4. About 15 to 20 minutes total, cover the pan and simmer the pasta until the extra liquid is absorbed and it is al dente, stirring every 5 minutes (see NOTES below).
5. Stir well, then top with lots of Parmesan cheese and serve right away.

NOTES

○   When your pasta has done cooking, remove the lid and continue cooking uncovered if your sauce is still too watery. By doing this, extra liquid can evaporate. This particular batch of one-pot spaghetti was cooked for 15 minutes with the lid on and 2 minutes without.

○   However, if your pasta isn't fully cooked by the time the sauce's surplus liquid has disappeared, stir a little more water and cook the dish until the noodles are tender yet firm.

○   Instead of using standard white pasta, you can substitute whole wheat or gluten-free spaghetti; however, you will need to increase the cooking time and/or liquid as previously mentioned.

ONE POT TOMATO BASIL PASTA

Prep time: 15 minutes

Cook time: 30 minutes

Total Time: 45 minutes

Servings: 6

INGREDIENTS

- 4 tablespoons of extra virgin olive oil, divided.
- 3 ounces of diced pancetta.
- 1 1/4 cups of yellow onion, chopped.
- 1 1/2 tablespoon of minced fresh garlic
- 2 3/4 cups of vegetable broth.
- 1 (28 oz) can tomatoes, diced.
- 1 1/2 tsp of Italian seasoning.
- 1/4 tsp of red pepper flakes.
- freshly ground black pepper and salt as needed.
- 3 3/4 cups (12 oz.) penne pasta.
- 1 1/2 cups (1.5 oz) of fresh spinach, chopped.
- 1/4 cup of fresh basil, chopped.
- 1 cup (2.2 oz) of finely parmesan.

INSTRUCTIONS

1. In a 5- or 6-quart pot, warm 2 Tbsp extra virgin olive oil over medium heat. Add the pancetta and saute for two minutes.
2. Add the onion and saute for 3 minutes. Saute for 30 more seconds after adding the garlic.
3. Add the tomato sauce, Italian seasoning, red pepper flakes, and salt and pepper to taste. Also add the veggie broth.
4. Turn up the heat to medium-high, simmer the sauce, and then stir in the pasta.

5. Medium-low heat should be used. 11 minutes should be enough time to cook the pasta with the lid on, stirring once halfway through.

6. Off the heat, let the dish rest for a few minutes before adding more broth if necessary.

7. Add the basil, 1/2 cup parmesan cheese, and spinach.

8. Sprinkle remaining 2 tablespoons of extra virgin olive oil over portions, then top with remaining 1/2 cup of parmesan.

ONE-POT PASTA BOLOGNESE

prep time: 5m

cook time: 25m

Servings: 4

INGREDIENTS

- 2 tbsp of olive oil.
- 1 diced onion.
- 2 diced carrots.
- 1 ribs celery, chopped
- 2 minced cloves garlic.
- 1/4 cup of tomato paste
- 1 lb. pf lean ground beef
- 1 (28 oz) can undrained tomatoes, diced.
- 2 tsp. of Italian seasoning.
- 1 lb. bucatini or fettuccine, uncooked
- 1/2 cup Parmesan cheese, freshly grated.
- 1/4 cup fresh parsley, chopped.
- freshly ground black pepper and Kosher salt as needed.

INSTRUCTION

1. In a big Dutch oven, warm the olive oil over medium-high heat. For about 5 minutes, add the onion, carrots, and celery and simmer until tender. For an additional minute, add the garlic.
2. After one more minute of cooking while stirring in the tomato paste, add the beef and season with salt and pepper. Cook for about 5 minutes, or until browned.
3. 3 cups of water, pasta, Italian spice, and tomatoes are added. To ensure that the pasta is fully submerged in liquid, stir everything together.
4. To prevent the pasta from sticking, bring to a boil and stir regularly. Cook for 10–12 minutes, or until pasta is al dente and sauce has thickened.

5. Salt and pepper to taste, then stir in the Parmesan and parsley.
6. Enjoy your dish while garnishing with more Parmesan and parsley.

ONE POT FETTUCCINE ALFREDO RECIPE

Prep Time: 5 Mins

Cook Time: 25 Mins

Total Time: 30 Mins

INGREDIENT

- 2 cups of milk
- 1 cup of chicken stock
- 8 ounces of dried Fettuccine
- 3 tablespoons of unsalted butter
- 2 minced garlic cloves.
- 1 teaspoon salt.
- 1/4 teaspoon of cracked black pepper.
- 1/5 cup parmesan cheese, grated.

INSTRUCTIONS

1. Put all the ingredients in a Dutch oven or a sizable pan except from the Parmesan.
2. Stir mixture in a pot over a medium-high heat until it boils. Should come to a boil in 4 to 5 minutes.
3. Once the liquid has to a boil, reduce the heat to medium and continue to simmer, stirring periodically, for 15 to 20 minutes, or when the pasta is al dente and most of the liquid has been absorbed.
4. Once the sauce is rich and creamy, remove it from the heat and stir the Parmesan. If you think the dish needs it, add more salt and pepper.
5. Serve pasta topped with more Parmesan.

NOTES

- You may limit how much salt is used in the dish and prevent over salination by using unsalted chicken stock (or broth).

- While still being slightly healthier than heavy cream, using full or partial fat milk will help to achieve a creamy and rich sauce.
- Throughout the simmering process, it's crucial to stir the meal regularly to ensure that the pasta cooks uniformly and doesn't stick to the bottom of the pot or to itself.

DUTCH OVEN PESTO PENNE

Cook Time: 25 mins

Total Time: 25 mins

Servings: 4

INGREDIENTS

- 2 cups of vegetable stock.
- 3 cups water, divided.
- 2 teaspoons of garlic powder
- 1 lb. of penne, Use gluten-free certified pasta as needed.
- 6 oz. of hot-smoked salmon.
- 6 oz. of basil pesto
- 2 tablespoons nutritional yeast.
- 12 oz. of jar quartered artichoke hearts, drained
- 1 cup halved cherry tomatoes
- 2 tbsp capers.

INSTRUCTIONS

1. To the Dutch oven, add stock, 2 cups water, and garlic powder. Place uncovered oven over coals. Soak broth for a while.
2. Pasta is added; stir. Make sure the pasta is submerged in water, and if necessary, add more broth or water.
3. Cook the pasta in the liquid until it is soft and most of the pasta has been absorbed (about 15 minutes, depending on the type of pasta and how hot your campfire is). While cooking, stir the pasta often, making careful to scrape the pot's bottom frequently to avoid sticking.
4. Pasta that sizzles indicates that it is clinging to the saucepan. To get rid of any pasta pieces that were trapped, add a little more water and stir.
5. Prepare the salmon as the pasta boils.
6. With a fork, flake the fish into pieces. Place aside. Discard the skin if the fillet has any.

7. Remove the pasta from the heat when it is tender. Add the last cup of water and stir.

8. Pasta should be combined with pesto and nutritional yeast.

9. Pasta should be topped with salmon, artichokes, tomatoes, and capers. To combine, stir. Serve right away.

10. Note

11. makes 6 smaller pieces or 4 substantial servings.

CHEESY BEEF & LENTIL PASTA BAKE WITH ROASTED VEG

Prep Time: 20 Min

Cook Time: 1 Hr. 10 Min

Total Time: 1 Hr. 30 Min

Servings: 4

INGREDIENT

Bolognese Sauce:

- 2 tablespoon of canola oil
- 1 chopped onion.
- 1 diced carrot, scrubbed.
- 1 stalk diced celery,
- 2 minced cloves garlic
- 1 lb. of lean ground beef
- 1 tablespoon Italian herb seasoning, dried
- 1½ teaspoon salt
- ¾ cup of red or white wine
- 1 can (28 oz) of crushed tomatoes
- ½ cup of dry green or brown lentils.
- 12 chopped fresh basil leaves

Roasted Vegetables:

- 2 tablespoon olive oil
- 2 finely chopped cloves garlic
- 1 tablespoon of dried Italian herb seasoning
- ½ teaspoon freshly ground black pepper and salt as needed.
- 3 cups of 2 zucchinis, cut into chunks.
- 1 large red bell pepper, cut into chunks.
- ½ medium eggplant, cut into chunks, unpeeled.

Pasta

- 1 pound of whole-grain penne
- 1 1/2 cups of mozzarella cheese, shredded.
- 3/4 cup of whole milk ricotta cheese

INSTRUCTION

- Over medium heat, warm the oil in a Dutch oven or sizable saucepan. Add the celery, onion, carrot, and garlic. Cook for 5 minutes, stirring frequently, or until softened. Crumble in the meat, sprinkle the heat up to medium-high, and season with salt and herbs. Cook for 5 minutes, stirring frequently and breaking up with a spoon, or until browned (do not drain).
- Add wine and simmer for 2 minutes. Add 2 cups of water, lentils, and tomatoes. Medium-low heat should be used. Stirring occasionally, simmer sauce for 35 to 40 minutes, or until thickened and lentils are thoroughly cooked. Stir in basil after removing from heat.
- Oven temperature should be set to 425°F (220°C). To line a baking sheet with a rim, use parchment paper. Toss the zucchini, bell pepper, and eggplant with the oil, garlic, herb seasoning, salt, and pepper in the large bowl. Vegetables should be transferred to the prepared baking sheet and roasted for 15 to 20 minutes, stirring once, or until tender.
- Prepare the pasta as directed on the package; drain, then add it back to the pot along with the prepared sauce and roasted veggies. Combine gently, then transfer to a round or rectangular (3.5 L) deep, oven-safe baking dish. Add slices of mozzarella and ricotta on top. Use foil to tent it loosely.
- Oven temperature is decreased to 375°F (190°C). Pasta dish should be baked for 20 to 25 minutes, or until the top is boiling and sticky. Before serving, allow to stand for five minutes.

NOTES

- Adapt the vegetable combination to the preferences of your family. Try Brussels sprouts, cauliflower, broccoli, or mushrooms.
- For a hotter version of the sauce, stir in a few hot pepper flakes.
- Use some prepared ingredients to speed up this recipe and have the meal on the table in less than an hour. Stir in 312 cups of premade marinara sauce after browning the steak and simmering it with wine. Add 1 can of rinsed lentils (14 oz/398 mL) and boil for 10 minutes. Over cooked noodles, spoon the roasted vegetables mixture. Ricotta should be topped with the dish instead of the mozzarella.

LASAGNA ROLL UPS

Total Time: 1 hr. 30 mins

Servings: 4

INGREDIENTS

- 1 oz. of ground beef
- 2 pounds of peeled and chopped tomatoes.
- 2 teaspoons of oregano, dried
- 2 teaspoon garlic powder
- freshly ground black pepper and salt as needed.
- 8 uncooked lasagna noodles
- 16 oz. of cottage cheese
- 1 oz. of freshly grated Parmesan cheese.
- 1 teaspoon of dried basil
- 8 oz. of shredded mozzarella cheese

INSTRUCTION

1. Over medium-high heat, add the ground beef to a Dutch oven or sizable saucepan. About 5 minutes of browning the ground beef while breaking it up with a spatula is required.
2. The beef should be cooked with the chopped tomatoes, oregano, garlic, 1 teaspoon salt, and 1/4 teaspoon black pepper for about 5 minutes, breaking up the tomatoes as you go.
3. Then, reduce the heat to medium-low and cover the pot. While the noodles are cooking, simmer, occasionally breaking up the tomatoes.
4. Follow the instructions on the package to prepare the lasagna noodles
5. Noodles should be drained and spread out flat on paper towels.
6. Set the oven to 425 °F.
7. In a mixing bowl, mix the cottage cheese, Parmesan, basil, 1/4 teaspoon of black pepper, and roughly HALF of the mozzarella until well combined.

8. Taste the sauce after removing it from the heat, and add salt and pepper as desired.

9. A small amount of the sauce should be spread on the bottom of a 9x13-inch baking dish

10. The cottage cheese mixture should be evenly spread over the top surface of the cooked lasagna noodles. The remaining sauce should be spread over the cheese mixture, followed by a tight roll that is placed seam-side down in the baking dish.

11. Then, top with the remaining mozzarella cheese and evenly sprinkle the remaining sauce over the rolled lasagna noodles

12. Aluminum foil the baking dish, and bake in the preheated oven for 30 minutes, or until bubbling

13. Bake the baking dish uncovered for five more minutes after removing the foil.

14. Before serving, let the lasagna roll-ups cool for about 10 minutes after removing them from the oven.

DUTCH OVEN BRAISED SLICED BEEF WITH MELTING ONIONS

Prep Time: 30 Mins

Cook Time: 3 Hrs.

Servings: 8

INGREDIENTS

- 5 pounds of beef lean cut.
- 3 pounds of onion
- 2 cups of chicken broth
- 7 teaspoon of vegetable oil
- freshly ground pepper ground
- salt as needed.

INSTRUCTIONS

1. Set your oven to 350 degrees (180 C).
2. Peel the onions, then slice them into 13-inch-thick pieces.
3. Onions should be sautéed in 2 tablespoons of vegetable oil in a large pan for 6 to 8 minutes over medium-high heat, or until golden brown. Add onions to the Dutch oven.
4. Get your beef ready. Eliminate the fat, connective tissues, and silver skin. Slice into 1/3–1/2-inch-thick pieces. Add lots of salt and freshly ground black pepper as needed.
5. Slices of beef should be seared for 2 minutes on each side over high heat in the same pan as the onions. For each batch, use 1 to 112 tbsp of oil. Transfer your meat to the Dutch oven once it has browned.
6. Pour chicken broth over the meat after deglazing the pan with it (simply add broth and mix for 1 minute over medium heat to dissolve scrapings).
7. Cook in the oven for 3 hours with the lid on your Dutch oven. After 2 hours, check and add water if necessary.

NOTES

- o Use duck or goose fat in place of the oil in this recipe if you really want to take it up a notch. I am aware that for some people, this is a massive no-no, therefore if you have never used a fat other than oil, avoid this advice.
- o However, if you're open to new experiences, go ahead and give it a shot. Both duck and goose fat have such a strong flavor that they both complement the dish's rich flavors quite well.
- o Sliced beef cooked in a Dutch oven keeps nicely for up to a week in the refrigerator.

CHAPTER 8: PORK

SWEET AND TANGY PORK CHOPS

Prep time: 10 mins

Cook time: 30 mins

Servings: 4

INGREDIENTS

- ½ cup of light brown sugar
- ¼ tsp. ground ginger
- ¼ tsp. ground cumin
- ¼ tsp. ground mustard
- ¼ tsp. freshly ground black pepper
- ½ tsp. salt
- 2 tbsp. soy sauce
- 6 boneless pork, loin chops
- 6 wooden (or metal) skewers

INSTRUCTION

1. To prepare a dry rub, combine the salt, mustard, black pepper, ginger, brown sugar, and cumin in a small bowl.
2. Put the soy sauce and pork chops in a 1-gallon zip-top bag and shake to coat the chops.
3. Chops should be taken out of the bag and given a dry massage on both sides.
4. When you're ready to transfer the pork chops to your cooler, place them in a 1-gallon resealable bag and place in the refrigerator.
5. Create a small fire and allow it to burn until hot coals or dim flames remain. Your cooking grate should be over the coals.
6. In order to skewer the chops at a diagonal, place the skewer through the top of one side of the pork loin chop and into the bottom corner of the opposite side. By doing this, the pork chop will remain stationary on the skewer.
7. Cook the skewers for 30 minutes, turning them over every 5 to 10 minutes, or until the juices flow clear. Serve warm.

NOTE

- o You can use bone-in pork chops in place of boneless pork chops. Prepare as directed above without the use of skewers, then when the food is done cooking, cover the bones in foil before serving.

CLASSIC PORK & BEANS

Prep Time: 10 Minutes

Cook Time: 6 Hours

Servings: 5

INGREDIENTS

- 14 lbs. of raw, dried navy beans, soaked in water overnight
- 8 oz. of salt pork, cut
- 10 garlic cloves, peeled and cut
- 1½ cups of onions, minced
- 1 cup of ketchup
- ¼ cup of corn syrup
- 3 sprigs thyme
- ½ tsp. mustard, dry
- Salt
- Black pepper, freshly ground

INSTRUCTION

1. the oven to 300 degrees Fahrenheit.
2. Cook the beans in boiling water in a Dutch oven for 20 minutes or until they are soft.
3. Drain.
4. Add the pork, ketchup, corn syrup, thyme, garlic, onions, and dry mustard. Salt and pepper the beans after covering them with water and seasoning. Cook for 6 hours with a cover in a preheated oven.

NOTE

- If you don't have any of the materials listed above, don't worry. There are only three ingredients called for in this recipe in an 1832 cookbook: a quart of beans, a pound of salt pork, and pepper.

PORK SHOULDER POT ROAST WITH WINTER VEGETABLES

Total Time: 12 hr. 30 min

Active: 1 hr.

Servings: 7

INGREDIENTS

- Kosher salt
- 4 lbs. of boneless pork shoulder
- 1/3 lb. of pancetta, cut
- 2 sprigs 6 leaves fresh sage
- 6 cloves garlic
- 2 carrots, peeled and cut into diced
- 1 rutabaga, peeled and cut into diced
- 1 turnip, peeled and cut into diced
- 1 large yellow onion, quartered
- 2 tbsp. tomato paste
- 1 tbsp. miso paste
- 1 sprig fresh rosemary
- 2 bottles (12 oz.) dark beer,
- 2 cups of chicken stock
- 1 tbsp. sherry vinegar
- Fresh mint, for garnish
- Fresh cilantro, for garnish
- Neutral oil, for frying
- 1 cup of fresh parsley leaves
- 1/4 cup of all-purpose flour
- 1 tsp. cayenne pepper
- 1 cup of onion rings, thinly sliced
- 1/2 cup of drained capers

INSTRUCTION

1. For the pork shoulder, season it heavily with salt the day before cooking, then place it in the refrigerator unwrapped.

2. Set the oven to 300 degrees Fahrenheit when you are ready to cook.

3. Cook the pancetta and 6 sage leaves in a large Dutch oven over medium heat for about 5 minutes, or until the pancetta renders its fat and becomes crispy. Sage and pancetta should be moved with a slotted spoon to a dish covered in paper towels and left to rest. In the pancetta fat, add the pork shoulder and brown it for roughly 5 minutes per side. Place aside.

4. Approximately 4 minutes after adding the garlic, sauté the carrots, rutabaga, turnips, and onion until browned. Cook for an additional minute before adding the tomato paste, miso paste, rosemary, and sage sprigs. Simmer after adding the beer and chicken stock. Add the sage and pancetta that was set aside back to the pan with the pork. For about 3 1/2 hours, cover and braise the food in the oven until fork-tender. 30 minutes should be given for the pork to rest in the liquid.

5. To make the fried parsley, fill a small saucepan with 1/2 inch of oil, and heat it to 350 degrees F over medium heat. Add the parsley leaves and cook for approximately a minute, or until crispy. Transfer with a slotted spoon to a dish covered in paper towels.

6. To make the fried onions, fill a small saucepan with 1/2 inch of oil, and heat it to 350 degrees F over medium heat.

7. In a small bowl, mix the flour and cayenne. Shake off any extra flour as you dredge the onions in it. Fry in batches for 3 to 5 minutes, or until browned. Transfer with a slotted spoon to a dish covered in paper towels.

8. Regarding the fried capers: With a paper towel, pat the capers dry. Oil should be added until the pan is half full. Turn the heat to medium after adding the capers to the cold oil. Cook for 3 to 5 minutes, or until the capers are crispy and cooked. Transfer with a slotted spoon to a dish covered in paper towels.

9. Transfer the pork to a cutting board after removing it from the liquid. Transferring the pork to a serving plate, slice it into 1-inch-thick pieces.

10. Add the vinegar to the braising liquid and stir. Place the fried capers, onions, parsley, mint, and cilantro on top of the sauce-covered pork.

PORK TENDERLOIN IN DUTCH OVEN RECIPE

Prep Time: 20 mins

Cook Time: 45 mins

Total Time: 1 hr. 5 minutes

Servings: 4

INGREDIENTS

- 1 pork (2 lbs.) tenderloin
- 1 tsp. sweet paprika
- 1 tsp. smoked paprika
- 1/2 tsp. garlic powder
- 3/4 tsp. fine sea salt or Kosher salt
- 1/2 tsp. ground black pepper
- 1.5 lb. potatoes
- 2 medium carrots (3.5 oz)
- 1 small red bell pepper (3.5 oz)
- 5 garlic cloves
- 1 medium onion (3.5 oz)
- 2 tbsp. vegetable oil
- 2 cups of low sodium chicken stock
- 9 oz. of green beans fresh and thawed
- 1 tsp. thyme, dried
- 1 tsp. dried rosemary

INSTRUCTIONS

1. Put the tenderloin on a cutting board and use a small, sharp knife to trim the fat and silverskin. Release a small amount of the skin before slipping the blade gently beneath it. With your other hand, grab this freed portion and slide the knife inside the skin while

keeping it at an angle away from the meat. Work carefully to only remove the skin and leave the underlying flesh in place. Next, divide the filet into two equal pieces.

2. Mix the garlic powder, salt, pepper, and smoked and sweet paprika. With the mixture, thoroughly rub the meat.

3. Vegetable preparation: Potatoes should be peeled and cut into 1-inch (or 1 12 cm) cubes. Carrots and pepper should also be cut into small cubes. Garlic cloves should be finely chopped and set aside. The onion should be chopped finely and kept apart from the other vegetables. Green beans should be cut in half and separated from the other ingredients.

4. In a large, shallow Dutch oven with 1 tablespoon of the oil heated, brown the meat for 2 minutes on each side. Take out of the pot. With a pinch of salt, sauté the onions in the remaining oil over medium heat for 2 minutes, stirring often.

5. Cooking vegetables: Add the other ingredients—all but the green beans—to the saucepan, mix thoroughly, and scrape the bottom as necessary. Vegetables should be cooked for 5 minutes with frequent stirring until somewhat softer. If necessary, add a splash of the chicken stock to prevent the veggies from catching.

6. Stir the remaining stock, the green beans, the thyme, and the rosemary. Place the two slices of pork on top. Cook for 15-20 minutes or until the internal temperature reaches 63 degrees Celsius/145 degrees Fahrenheit with the lid on and the heat reduced (Note 2). While you finish preparing the dish, remove the meat from the saucepan and allow it to rest.

7. For an additional 5 minutes, simmer the vegetables and gravy with the cover on. To enable the sauce to thicken and the potatoes to soften, remove the lid and simmer for an additional 5 minutes (if they are not already).

8. Slice the meat, place it atop the potatoes and vegetables, and then serve.

NOTES

o When the sauce is reduced, the dish could become too salty if you don't use homemade or low sodium chicken stock.

o The meat must not be cooked past this point or it will turn chewy and dry. Don't overcook the meat.

JERK PORK CHOPS WITH PLANTAINS

Prep Time: 1 1/4 Hr.

Cook Time: 35 Min.

Servings: 7

INGREDIENTS

- 8 pork chops
- 4 tbsp. extra-virgin olive oil and 2 tbsp. onion powder
- 2 tsp. thyme
- 1 tsp. ground allspice
- ½ tsp. ground cumin
- 2 tsp. sea salt, divided
- 4 lbs. of ripe plantains, peeled and cut into thick slices
- ½ cup of honey
- 1 tsp. of salt.
- Rub the pork chops evenly with the 4 tbsp. of olive oil, onion powder, thyme, allspice, cumin, and 1 tsp of salt.

INSTRUCTION

1. Set the oven to 350 degrees Fahrenheit.
2. The last drop of olive oil should be heated in a Dutch oven over medium heat. Cook the pork chops for about 4 minutes after adding half of them. Once the pork has lightly browned on all sides, flip it over and cook for another 4 minutes. Repeat with the remaining chops after removing them to a dish. Remove all of the fat. To remain warm, cover.
3. In the Dutch oven, mix the plantains, butter, honey, and the final teaspoon of salt. Bake for 20 minutes, rotating once, until soft and browned, covered, in a preheated oven. Serve the pork chops alongside.

NOTES

- o Plantains, which contain more starch and less sugar than bananas, are frequently used in Caribbean cuisine in place of pasta and potatoes. They are offered all year long and are sold in the supermarket's fresh vegetable area.
- o In contrast to bananas, plantains are cooked before eating and are classified as vegetables rather than fruits.

SHREDDED PORK BURRITOS

Prep Time: 10 Mins

Cook Time: 4 1/2 Hrs.

Servings: 7

INGREDIENTS

For the pork

- 1 chopped large onion
- 4 crushed cloves garlic
- 1 bone-in pork shoulder (4.5 lbs.)
- 1 tbsp. coriander seeds
- 1 tbsp. cumin seeds
- 2 tbsp. oregano leaves, dried
- 3 canned chipotle chiles
- 2 bay leaves
- Salt

For serving

- warmed corn tortillas,
- Salsa for garnish
- Lime wedges; for garnish
- Sliced avocados; for garnish
- Chopped cilantro; for garnish

INSTRUCTION

1. Set the oven's temperature to 450 degrees Fahrenheit.
2. The onion, garlic, pork, coriander, cumin, oregano, chipotle chiles, and bay leaves should all be combined in a Dutch oven. Add enough water to the meat to cover it. Place in a

covered pan over medium-high heat and bring to a boil. Simmer at a lower temperature until the meat separates from the bone (3 to 4 hours).

3. Onto a dish, remove the meat. Place the container with the broth aside.

4. The meat should now be placed back in the Dutch oven and heated oven. Bay leaves should be thrown away once the meat has browned in the oven.

5. With two forks, coarsely shred the pork, removing any fat. Use salt to season. Place a generous amount of the meat mixture inside each tortilla. Garnish with salsa, lime wedges, avocados, and/or cilantro.

NOTES

○ Because the pig broth is so good, we advise saving some for subsequent use in soups and stews. Use a spoon to scrape off any surface fat after pouring it off, then put it in the fridge or freezer.

PORK LOIN BRAISED IN MILK

Prep Time: 5 Mins

Cook Time: 1 Hr.

Total Time: 1 Hr. 5 Mins

Servings: 6

INGREDIENTS

- 1 1/2 pounds of boneless center-cut pork loin
- freshly ground black pepper and Salt
- 1 tbsp. olive oil
- 3 tbsp. butter, divided
- 1 bunch roughly chopped fresh sage, 5 large leaves
- 1 cup of whole milk, 3.5%
- 1 cup of heavy cream, 35%
- Strips of zest from 1/3 of a lemon

INSTRUCTION

1. In a medium Dutch oven with a heavy bottom, heat oil and 1 tablespoon of the butter over medium-high heat until butter melts. Add the pork, fat side down, and heat for 2-3 minutes per side, or until browned on all sides.

2. Remove fat from the casserole, lower the heat to medium, and then stir in the final 2 tablespoons of butter. Add half of the sage leaves when the butter has melted, and cook for a few seconds. Add milk and cream gradually (**Hands well back as it may steam and spatter! Add the lemon zest, add a little salt and pepper, and boil. Turn the pork over after 30 minutes while you lower the heat to medium-low to low and slowly simmer the dish for 45 to 1 hour. Add a little warm water if the liquid level in the pot becomes too low. Using a meat thermometer, check the doneness of the meat starting at about 45–50 minutes of cooking. When it hits 145–150° F, it is finished. On a chopping board, transfer the meat, and cover with foil. Lie down.

3. Meanwhile, stir in the remaining sage leaves and scrape the pan's bottom with a wooden spoon to dislodge the browned goodness there. The gravy will progressively darken and thicken as you proceed. Add a little more milk to thin it out if it becomes too thick. After tasting, add salt and pepper as desired.

4. After the meat has rested for about ten minutes, slice it thinly and arrange it on a serving platter. Over the meat, spoon heated sauce.

HAWAIIAN KALUA PIG

Prep Time: 15 Mins

Cook Time: 6 Hrs.

Total Time: 6 Hrs. 15 Minutes

Servings: 6

INGREDIENTS

- 3 1/2 lbs. of Boneless Pork Shoulder
- 2–3 tablespoons of Hawaiian Sea Salt
- 1 teaspoon of Fresh Ground Pepper
- 3 tablespoons Vegetable Oil
- 3 tablespoons Liquid Smoke
- 12 oz. can Guava Juice
- 1/2 cup of Water

INSTRUCTIONS

1. One hour before cooking, take the pork shoulder out of the refrigerator to let it loosen up and ensure equal cooking. On each side, sprinkle salt and pepper.
2. Oven should be heated to 300 degrees.
3. Vegetable oil is added to the Dutch oven, which is placed over a burner at medium heat, and heated until shimmering. The pork should be seared until golden brown on all sides. Make sure to wait until the pig releases from the pan naturally before moving to a new side to sear.
4. Sprinkle with guava juice, water, and liquid smoke. Put the pork in the oven covered. To bast pork, uncover every hour.
5. When the pork easily shreds with two forks, take it out of the oven after 5 to 6 hours. After removing from the oven, allow it cool for 20 minutes before shredding completely. Serve while still warm.

DUTCH OVEN PORK ROAST WITH GRAVY

Prep Time: 15 mins

Cook Time: 1 hr. 45 mins

Resting Time: 15 mins

Total Time: 2 hrs. 15 mins

Servings: 6

INGREDIENTS

- ⅓ cup of all-purpose flour
- Salt and pepper as needed.
- 4 pounds of boneless pork loin roast
- 1 tbsp. of butter
- 2 tbsp. of olive oil
- 2 cups of chicken broth, divided
- 5 carrots, peeled and cut.
- 2 thinly sliced onions
- 4 large ribs celery, cut into crescents.
- 2 minced cloves garlic
- 1 cup of apple cider.
- 4 fresh thyme sprigs.
- 4 fresh rosemary sprigs
- 2 bay leaves
- 3 medium Russet potatoes, peeled and cut.
- 2 tbsp. of butter
- 2 tbsp. of all-purpose flour
- 1 - 1 ½ cups of juices

INSTRUCTIONS

1. Set the oven to 350°F.

2. On a piece of wax paper, mix the flour with plenty of salt and pepper. Toss the roast in the flour mixture and pat it dry.

3. A large Dutch oven should be heated over medium-high heat until the butter and oil are hot but not smoking. The pork should be seared on all four sides for 4-6 minutes, or just long enough for the meat to turn a lovely golden brown and easily release from the pan. The meat won't need to be fully cooked because it will finish in the oven. Toss the pork onto a platter.

4. In order to deglaze the pan, turn the heat down to medium, add 1 cup of the chicken stock, and stir with a wooden spoon (loosening all of the browned bits from the bottom). To the pot, add the carrots, onion, celery, and garlic. Cook the onions while stirring until they are transparent (about 10 minutes).

5. Stack the vegetables on top of the pork. Add the apple cider, bay leaves, thyme, rosemary, and the remaining 1 cup of chicken broth. For a total of around 70-80 minutes, season with salt and pepper, cover, and bake in the 350°F oven (about 20 minutes per pound). During the last 40 to 45 minutes, add the potatoes to the pot and stir them into the broth. Once the potatoes are tender and the meat reaches an internal temperature of 145 °F, cover the dish and put it back in the oven for the remaining 40 to 45 minutes.

6. Prior to slicing and serving, give the pork a 10-15 minute rest.

7. Juices and drips from the saucepan should be strained. In a skillet, heat the butter until it bubbles up. After adding the flour, stir for 30 seconds. Juices should be added gradually while whisking continuously until the gravy achieves the appropriate consistency.

8. While the gravy bubbles and cooks for 1-2 minutes, continue whisking. To taste, add more salt and pepper to the seasoning.

NOTES

o To protect the pork roast from drying out, cook it in the Dutch oven with the lid on. This will preserve the moisture in the pot. The ideal result is juicy and tender!

o Since the Dutch oven's effective heat frequently shortens the cooking time, check the meat early. The boneless pork loin roast should be cooked at 350° F for roughly 20 minutes per pound as a general guideline. A 4-lb. roast might be prepared in as little as 70 minutes, though.

- o Depending on the size, thickness, and temperature of your pork when it goes into the oven, the entire cooking time will vary. As a result, the easiest way to determine when your pork has reached 145°F is to use a meat thermometer.
- o Before slicing and serving, allow the meat to rest. By doing this, the fluids will be able to circulate rather than simply run onto the cutting board.
- o To finish, garnish with finely chopped fresh herbs for a vibrant accent.

CHILI VERDE PORK

Total Time: 1 hr. 40 min

Prep Time: 10 min

Cook Time: 1 hr. 30 min

Servings: 12

INGREDIENTS

- 4 lbs. of pork butt, cut into cubes
- 4 chopped yellow onions
- 4 Anaheim chiles
- 2 minced jalapeno
- 4 tbsp. of chopped garlic
- 1 lb. of tomatillos
- 1/2 cup of white wine
- 1/4 cup of white vinegar
- 1 cup of chicken stock
- 2 tbsp. of ground oregano
- 2 tbsp. of ground cumin
- 1 tbsp. of salt
- 1 tbsp. of ground black pepper

INSTRUCTION

1. Heat the oil in a medium Dutch oven before adding the onion, peppers, and garlic. Don't let it brown; saute until transparent. Remove and reserve the mixture.
2. On an open heat, carefully grill the tomatillos until they are lightly browned. Take off of the heat, put in a bowl, and wrap in plastic to keep warm for 20 minutes.
3. Dutch oven with pork butt added; cook over high heat until browned on all sides.

4. To the pork, add the onion-pepper mixture and tomatillos. Mix completely, then use vinegar and white wine to deglaze. Add chicken stock, oregano, cumin, salt, and pepper after reducing for 5 minutes.
5. 1 hour of simmering is recommended.

CHAPTER 9: SANDWICH

KOREAN-INSPIRED BRISKET SANDWICHES WITH SESAME COLESLAW

Prep time: 45 mins

Cook time: 4hr

Total time: 6hr

Servings: 8

INGREDIENTS

For the brisket

- 4-5 lbs. of brisket lightly trimmed of excess fat
- 1 1/2 tbsp. of kosher salt as needed.
- 1 tbsp. of garlic powder
- 1 tbsp. of onion powder
- 2 tbsp. of red chile powder

For the sauce

- 2 tbsp. of mild vegetable oil
- 11 oz. of Spanish onion, finely chopped
- 7 large minced cloves garlic.
- 2 tbsp. of fresh ginger, grated
- 1 cup of dry red wine
- 3 cups of homemade chicken stock.
- 1/4 cup of homemade spicy chili paste
- 1/2 cup of ketchup
- 2 tbsp. of soy sauce
- 3 tbsp. of brown sugar
- 1 tbsp. of Worcestershire sauce
- 1 tbsp. of fish sauce
- 1 tbsp. of cornstarch

For the coleslaw

- 3 cups of napa cabbage, finely shredded
- 2 cups of red cabbage, finely shredded

- 1 tsp. of kosher salt
- 1 tbsp. of toasted sesame oil
- 2 tbsp. of rice vinegar, unseasoned
- 1/4 cup of mayonnaise
- 3 finely sliced scallions
- 2 tbsp. of toasted sesame seeds

For serving

- sandwich rolls or Potato buns
- 3 small thinly sliced Persian cucumbers

INSTRUCTION

Make the brisket:

1. In order for the brisket to fit inside your Dutch oven, you may need to chop it into two or more pieces.
2. Mix the salt, gochugaru, onion powder, and garlic powder in a small bowl. Place the brisket on a large platter, liberally sprinkle the rub over the beef, and then press it into the meat. Depending on the size of the brisket, you might not need all of it.
3. The brisket can either be refrigerated for up to 24 hours or left at room temperature for 1 hour.
4. The oven should be preheated to 275°F (135°C) with a rack in the lower middle position.

Make the sauce:

5. In a large Dutch oven, heat the oil over medium-high heat. Stirring occasionally, add the onion, garlic, and ginger. Cook for 5 to 7 minutes, or until the onion turns tender and golden.
6. Stir the wine, stock, gochujang, ketchup, soy sauce, brown sugar, Worcestershire sauce, and fish sauce by stirring everything together. To the Dutch oven, add the brisket. Between one-half and three-quarters of the way up the meat, the liquid should be. If necessary, add more water or stock. The liquid should come to a boil.
7. Slide the Dutch oven into the oven while it is covered. Cook the brisket for about 3 1/2 hours, monitoring it every hour and spooning braising liquid on top. For the final hour of cooking, remove the lid.
8. In order to keep the beef warm, transfer it to a plate or cutting board with a rim.
9. The sauce should be simmered in the Dutch oven for about 20 minutes, or until it has been reduced to 3 cups (it will thicken more as it cools). Add a cornstarch slurry to the sauce to make it thicker if you choose. Stir the cornstarch and 2 teaspoons (30 ml) of

cold water in a small bowl. Stir in half of the slurry as the sauce simmers. Add the second half of the slurry if the sauce still needs to be thickened.

10. We prefer to prepare the brisket a full day in advance (or up to 3 days). Restock the Dutch oven with the unsliced beef and chill it overnight. The sauce's solid fat can be removed from the top fairly easily once it has cooled. Take the brisket out of the sauce and slice it against the grain while it is still cool if you prefer thin, orderly slices. Place the slices back in the sauce-filled pot, turn the heat to low, and simmer the food until it is well heated. Additionally, you can reheat the sliced brisket in the Dutch oven for about 15 minutes at 275°F (135°C) until it is hot.

11. Allow the brisket to rest for at least 20 minutes before slicing it if you're serving it that day. Make sure to cut against the grain using a sharp knife. You can see the muscle fibers going in one direction if you look at the brisket. These fibers are shortened by cutting across them, resulting in soft flesh. No matter how you cook the brisket, it will be stringy and difficult to chew if you slice against the grain.) Skim the fat from the sauce using a spoon or a fat separator.

Make the coleslaw:

12. Combine the cabbages in a large bowl and season with salt.
13. Mix the sesame oil, rice vinegar, and mayonnaise in a small bowl. Toss the cabbage with the dressing, scallions, and sesame seeds after adding them.
14. To assemble the dish, place some beef on a bun, top with sauce, then add coleslaw and cucumbers, if preferred. Keep a lot of napkins on hand.

SEAFOOD FISH SANDWICH

INGREDIENT

Fish:

- 4 fish filets
- ½ cup of flour
- 1 cup of vegetable oil.
- 2 cups of bread crumbs
- 2 medium-sized eggs
- 1 cup of beer
- ½ tsp. of paprika
- ½ tsp. of cayenne pepper
- 1 tsp. of baking powder

Tartar Sauce:

- 1/2 cup of mayonnaise
- 1 shallot
- 2 tbsp. of dill
- 1/4 cup of pickle chips
- 2 tbsp. capers
- A touch of soy sauce

INSTRUCTION

Tartar Sauce:

1. It is not too difficult to make tartar sauce. To make the tartar sauce, mix the mayonnaise, finely diced pickle chips, shallot, capers, dill, and soy sauce in a bowl. As desired, add salt.

Fish:

2. Pre-heat your oil to 350° using a deep fryer, Dutch oven, or saucepan with a heavy bottom. Afterward, combine 1 cup of flour with 1 teaspoon each of salt, paprika, cayenne, corn starch, baking powder, and black and white pepper.
3. Pour in your cup of beer and stir the mixture some more. Put the remaining 1/2 cup of flour into a shallow bowl or plate right now.
4. Each fish filet should be well-seasoned with salt and pepper before being floured. After that, dip the fish into the batter, making care to coat all sides.

5. Your filets should fry for 8 to 10 minutes after being carefully placed in the oil. When the fish is golden in color and feels crispy, it is finished. You might need to flip the filets occasionally to make sure they cook evenly.

DUTCH OVEN HOT HAM SANDWICHES

Prep Time: 10 mins

Cook Time: 20 mins

Total Time: 30 mins

INGREDIENTS

- 1 Italian Loaf
- ½-1 lb. of sliced ham
- ½-1 lb. cheese, sliced
- Condiments as needed

INSTRUCTIONS

1. To prepare the coals, heat your wood or charcoal. Make sure you give yourself enough time to complete this because it will take some time. For this recipe, roughly 40 briquets are required.
2. Remember that this is a pull-apart bread and do not cut all the way through when slicing your bread into 1-inch slices.
3. Put your ham, cheese, and whatever else you wish to add in every other piece.
4. Place in your dutch oven after wrapping in tinfoil. The Dutch oven's lid should be placed there.
5. 20 coals should be added to the fire pit's base. They should be uniformly distributed to fill your Dutch oven.
6. Immediately set the Dutch oven over the coals.
7. Next, sprinkle the top with the final 20 embers.
8. Check after around 20 minutes of cooking.
9. The bread and cheese only need to be warmed up.
10. Remove it from the stove once it has finished cooking.
11. Now relax and take pleasure. You merit it.

FRENCH DIP SANDWICHES

Prep Time: 10 Mins

Cook Time: 2 Hrs. 30 Mins

Total Time: 2 Hrs. 40 Mins

Servings: 6

INGREDIENTS

- 3 pounds of chuck roast, extra fat removed
- 5 thinly sliced yellow onions
- 6 pressed cloves garlic,
- 1 tbsp. of butter
- 2 tbsp. of kosher salt
- 2 tbsp. of freshly cracked black pepper
- ½ tsp. of sugar
- 28 ounces of beef stock
- 6 hoagie rolls
- 12 slices of provolone, havarti, or Swiss cheese

INSTRUCTION

1. Set oven to 325 degrees Fahrenheit (165 degrees C).
2. The onion slices should be arranged in a layer at the bottom of a 9 x 13 baking dish or a large Dutch oven. Slices of onion are seasoned with the sugar, 1 teaspoon of salt, and 1 teaspoon of pepper.
3. To prepare a garlic paste, combine the pressed garlic with 1 teaspoon each of salt and black pepper in a small bowl. The remaining salt and pepper should be used to season the meat well on both sides before applying the garlic paste. In your baking dish or Dutch oven, layer the seasoned onion slices with the seasoned chuck.
4. Place in the oven for 2 hours after adding beef broth or consommé. After 2 hours, for 30 to 1 hour, until the chuck roast is soft and just just holding together, tent with aluminum foil or cover with an oven-safe lid.
5. Take the roast out and cut and shred it on a cutting board. Separate the onions from the jus using a fine mesh sieve, then store the jus and onions separately.

6. Slices of cheese, onions, and meat should be layered within hoagie rolls. Put the items on baking sheets and turn on the still-warm oven. After the cheese has melted, turn off the oven.
7. Jus should be available on the side for dipping.

NOTE

o   Instead of using a baking pan and foil, you can use a cast iron Dutch oven with a lid.

HEARTY ITALIAN SANDWICHES

Prep Time: 20 mins.

Cook Time: 3 hrs.

Servings: 8

INGREDIENTS

- 1-1/2 lbs. of lean ground beef
- 1-1/2 lbs. of bulk Italian sausage
- 2 large sliced onions
- 2 sliced large green peppers
- 2 sliced large sweet red peppers
- 1 tsp. salt
- 1 tsp. pepper
- 1/4 tsp. crushed red pepper flakes
- 8 sandwich rolls, split and toasted
- Monterey Jack cheese, Shredded

INSTRUCTION

1. Cook the beef and sausage in a Dutch oven over medium heat until neither is pink anymore and crumble them both. In a 5-qt. slow cooker, layer a third of the onions and peppers with the beef mixture. Layer again, then add the final vegetables. Sprinkle salt, pepper, and pepper flakes to taste.
2. Vegetables should be soft after 3 to 4 hours of cooking on low with the cover on. Serve around 1 cup of the meat and vegetables on each bun using a slotted spoon. Adding cheese on top is optional. If desired, use pan juices as a dipping sauce.

HOT BEEF SANDWICHES

Cook time: 1hr 10 mins

Servings: 5

INGREDIENT

- 1 tbsp. lard or shortening
- 4 -5 lbs. chuck roast boneless
- 5 peeled garlic cloves
- 1 sliced onion
- 2 cups of water
- 1 tbsp. Kitchen Bouquet
- 2 tsp. of black pepper
- 1 tbsp. of salt
- 2 tbsp. of cornstarch
- 1⁄2 cup of water

INSTRUCTION

1. Set the oven's temperature to 350.
2. In a Dutch oven or other heavy-bottomed pot with a lid, melt the lard over high heat.
3. All sides of the roast with salt and pepper.
4. Place the roast in the saucepan after the lard begins to emit a "hot" odor.
5. To help seal in the juices, grill the roast for 1 minute on each side.
6. Around the roast, scatter onion slices and garlic cloves, and stir to lightly brown them (but not caramelize).
7. Add 2 cups of water to the Kitchen Bouquet and mix. Over the roast, pour the water mixture. up to a boil.
8. Place in the bottom of the oven with a tight cover. 1 hour of roasting. Turn the roast over halfway through the roasting process.
9. When the roast is finished, put it on a dish and shield it with foil to keep it warm (actually hot). Reset the Dutch oven to medium heat on the stove.

10. Mix 1/2 cup water and cornstarch. While crushing the garlic cloves, stir into the Dutch oven. Season to taste and bring to a boil. Take out of the stove.
11. Serve the roast on toast with mashed potatoes after slicing it and placing it back in the Dutch oven.
12. Enjoy.

CHAPTER 10: PIZZA

ONE POT PIZZA PASTA

Prep Time: 10 Mins

Cook Time: 20 Mins

Servings: 8

INGREDIENTS

- 1 pound of lean ground beef.
- 5 oz. mini pepperoni
- 1 finely chopped yellow onion.
- 1 green pepper, finely chopped
- 2 cloves garlic.
- ¼ tsp. salt
- ¼ tsp. black pepper
- 14.75 oz. (1 can) of beef broth
- 14 oz. (1 jar) of pizza sauce
- 1 cup of water
- 2 tbsp. of tomato paste
- 2 tsp. of Italian seasoning
- 1 tsp. basil, dried
- 3 cups of small shell pasta
- 2 cups of mozzarella cheese, shredded

INSTRUCTIONS

1. The ground beef, small pepperoni, green pepper, onion, garlic, and salt should all be placed in a big frying pan with high sides and a lid. until the beef is no longer pink, cook and crumble (about 5-7 minutes). From the skillet, remove any extra fat.
2. Add the basil, tomato paste, Italian seasoning, water, pizza sauce, and beef broth. up to a boil.
3. Add the dry small shell pasta and bring to a boil once more. When the pot reaches a rolling boil, cover it with the lid and lower the heat to medium. For 20 minutes, cook.
4. All of the water should have been absorbed after 20 minutes of cooking. If not, simmer it (covered) for a little while longer.

5. Stir in the grated cheese, letting it melt into the pasta. Serve right away!

NOTES

- o You can definitely get 8 servings from this dish if you're feeding a family or simply tweens. Plan on 6 servings if you are serving only adult-sized amounts.
- o In addition, you can substitute 1 cup of chopped pepperoni for the small pepperoni.

ONE POT PIZZA CASSEROLE

INGREDIENTS

- 1 tbsp. of olive oil
- 1 lb. of Italian sausage casings removed
- 2 minced cloves garlic
- 1 diced green pepper
- 1/2 tsp. of salt
- 1/4 tsp. of black pepper
- 29 oz. of crushed tomatoes
- 2 cups of chicken broth
- 1/2 tbsp. basil, dried
- 1/2 tbsp. oregano, dried
- 1/2 tsp. of crushed red pepper flakes
- 8 oz. rotini
- 2 cups of mozzarella, shredded
- Pepperoni for topping
- For topping sliced olives
- For topping shredded parmesan

INSTRUCTIONS

1. Set the oven's temperature to 350.
2. Over medium heat, warm the oil in a large oven-safe skillet. As you cook, crumble in the Italian sausage. Add the green pepper and garlic once it has completely broken up but before it starts to brown. Add salt and pepper to taste. About 5 to 7 minutes of sautéing should result in the peppers starting to soften.
3. Combine in the chicken broth, oregano, basil, red pepper flakes, and smashed tomatoes.
4. Add rotini and stir. Stirring regularly, bring to a boil, then reduce heat and simmer for 10 to 15 minutes (or until the rotini only has a slight bite to it).
5. Add 1/2 cup of the mozzarella and stir. Add the remaining cheese, pepperoni, and olives on top. Cook it for 5 to 10 minutes, or until the cheese has melted, in a preheated oven.

ONE POT PEPPERONI PIZZA ORZO

Prep Time: 5 Mins

Cook Time: 25 Mins

Servings: 4

INGREDIENTS

- 2 tbsp. of olive oil
- 1 finely chopped shallot,
- 3 minced garlic cloves,
- 9 oz. of orzo pasta
- 2 1/2 cups of chicken broth
- 1 tbsp. of tomato paste
- 1 cup of tomato purée
- 3.5 oz. of roasted peppers, drained, from a jar
- 1 oz. of Parmesan, grated.
- 6.5 oz. of mozzarella, grated.
- 3.5 oz. of thin pepperoni, slices
- basil leaves
- 1/2 tsp. of crushed red pepper flakes
- Spices as needed.
- 1 tsp. of oregano, thyme, sage, salt, and black pepper, dried.

INSTRUCTION

1. Before you begin cooking, do all of the preparations: finely cut the shallot and mince the garlic.
2. An oven-safe nonstick skillet with oil is heated over medium-low heat. Add the shallot and garlic, and sauté for approximately 2 minutes, or until tender and aromatic. For one minute, add orzo and toast. Stir the spices and toast for 30 seconds, or until fragrant. Bring to a boil after adding the broth. Stir in the tomato paste until it has dissolved. Add tomato purée and thoroughly stir. With the lid on, cook the orzo for 10 minutes over low heat, tossing regularly to keep it from adhering to the pan's bottom. If necessary, include more water or chicken broth.

3. The oven should be preheated to 200 °C/400 °F in the interim.
4. Cut the heat when you're ready. Stir in the grated Parmesan and the roasted peppers. then sprinkle fresh basil leaves, pepperoni, and shredded mozzarella on top. Add some black pepper and red pepper flakes to finish.
5. Bake for 10 minutes, or until the cheese is melted and the top is golden brown. Serve right away with a substantial side salad. Enjoy!

ONE POT MUSHROOM PIZZA ORZO

Prep Time: 5 Mins

Cook Time: 25 Mins

Total Time: 30 Mins

Servings: 4

INGREDIENTS

- 2 tbsp. of extra-virgin olive oil
- 10 oz. of baby bella mushrooms, sliced.
- ½ diced yellow onion,
- 2 minced garlic cloves.
- 1 tbsp. of balsamic vinegar
- 1 can (28 oz) of whole peeled tomatoes
- 14 oz of water
- 1 tsp salt
- 1/4 tsp crushed red pepper flakes
- 1/2 tsp oregano, dried
- 3/4 cup of orzo
- 4 oz. of sliced fresh mozzarella.
- for garnish fresh parsley.

INSTRUCTIONS

1. A large oven-safe skillet should be filled with olive oil. Over medium, the oil is heated.
2. The mushrooms should be added once the oil is shimmering and cooked for 7 to 10 minutes, until caramelized on all sides. The mushrooms should be taken out and left aside.
3. Turn the heat down to medium or low. Put the onion in. For 2 minutes, cook. Balsamic vinegar and garlic are added. Mix everything together and combine any caramelized bits from the pan's bottom.
4. Mix the water and tomatoes together. Slice the tomatoes into tiny pieces using the side of a wooden spoon. Mix the orzo, salt, oregano, and red pepper flakes.
5. Simmer for a while. Orzo should be simmered uncovered for 7-9 minutes while being stirred occasionally to prevent the pasta from sticking to the bottom.

6. When the orzo is al dente, sprinkle cheese and mushrooms on top.
7. Turn your broiler to high. For a few minutes, place the skillet under the broiler to melt the cheese.
8. Add extra red pepper flakes and fresh parsley that has been cut on top.

ONE-POT PIZZA RIGATONI RECIPE

Prep Time: 5 Mins

Cook Time: 25 Mins

Servings: 6

INGREDIENTS

- 1 box (1 lb.) of rigatoni pasta noodles
- 1 jar (24 oz.) of marinara sauce
- ½ cup water
- ½ cup of diced red onion
- 1 diced bell pepper
- 2 minced cloves garlic
- 2 tbsp. of Italian seasoning
- 1 package (7 oz.) pepperoni, slices
- 1 bag (8 oz.) of mozzarella cheese, shredded
- For topping, Pepperoncini peppers

INSTRUCTION

1. Chop up the garlic. Bell pepper and onion should be diced. Quarter two-thirds of the pepperoni slices in the package.
2. Set the stove's heat to medium. Add the minced garlic after cooking spraying a Dutch oven or saucepan with a high wall. Garlic is cooked till golden.
3. Cook the bell peppers and onion dice after adding them. Add the pepperoni chunks and stir.
4. Fill the pot with the entire box of noodles. Add the Italian spice, a half cup of water, and the marinara sauce container on top. Stir thoroughly.
5. Increase the heat to medium-high while the pot is covered. Cook for about 20 minutes, stirring every so often.
6. Stir half of the cheese bag into the cooked, soft noodles. The remaining intact pepperoni slices and cheese should be added to the pasta. Put the pot's lid back on and let the cheese melt.
7. Pepperoncini peppers or other toppings are served on top of the pizza rigatoni as preferred.

I appreciate you taking the time to read this book and trying the recipes.

I sincerely hope you have enjoyed reading the book and experimenting with the recipes as much as I have enjoyed creating it.

Made in the USA
Middletown, DE
07 October 2023

40383562R00113